VENISON COOKBOOK WITH DELICIOUS RECIPES

Steven Sommers

Table of Contents

Venison Steaks With Scotch Sour Sauce

Yield: 4 servings

2 tb butter, divided use

1/4 c finely chopped shallots

5 cranberries, crushed

1/4 c scotch whiskey

3/4 c orange juice

2 tb lemon juice

2 tb red currant jelly

1 ts dijon mustard

2 ts cornstarch

2 tb water

4 venison porterhouse steaks

1 or 4 small beef porterhouse

1 steaks

Combine 1 tbsp. butter, shallots and berries in a 2 cup glass measure. Cover with vented plastic wrap. Microwave on high for 2 minutes. Add Scotch whiskey and microwave on high 1 minute or until boiling. Stir in orange juice, lemon juice, jelly and mustard. Microwave on high 2 minutes or until boiling. Combine cornstarch with water. Stir into sauce;microwave on high 1 minute or until boiling;set aside. Preheat a microwave browning dish according to the maximum time given in manufacturer's directions. Rub remaining 1 tbsp. butter over surface. Immediately, press venison or beef onto hot surface. When brown, turn over. Microwave on high 2 minutes or to desired doneness. Do not overcook. Serve immediately with sauce.

Barbecued Venison Ribs

Categories: game, barbeque

Yield: 6 servings

2 1/2 c water

3 c ketchup

1 tb white vinegar

1/4 c lemon juice

1/2 c worcestershire sauce

1/2 c 100% wisconsin maple syrup

1/2 c brown sugar

2 md onions, diced

2 tb chili powder

1/2 ts salt

6 lb venison ribs with some loin

1 meat attached

1 freshly ground black pepper

1 to taste

Preheat oven to 325 degrees. In large bowl, combine all ingredients except ribs and pepper. Blend well. Sprinkle ribs with pepper and additional salt. Place in 5 qt. roasting pan in double layer. Roast 1 hour. Pour sauce over ribs. Increase heat to 350 degrees and bake until ribs just begin to char on top, about 1 1/2 hours. Turn ribs over cover pan and bake about 30 minutes longer, until ribs are tender and sauce is thick. To serve, place ribs on serving platter. Pour sauce over ribs. Makes about 6 servings.

Note: If venison is a little gamey tasting, increase vinegar in sauce to 3 tbsp. . Taste sauce after mixing and add additional brown sugar to taste, about 1/2 cup.

Venison Picadillo

Categories: game

Yield: 8 servings

3/4 c chopped onion

1 ts chopped garlic

2 tb olive oil

2 lb venison shoulder or leg, 1 ground

2 ts red chili flakes

1 ts dried oregano

1 ts ground cumin

1 ts ground coriander

1/2 ts ground cloves

2 c canned whole tomatoes,

1 seeded and chopped

2 tb red wine vinegar

2 tb raisins

1/4 ts salt

1/4 ts black pepper

In a large pan, saute onion and garlic in the oil until onion is golden. Add ground venison, chili flakes, oregano, cumin, coriander and cloves. Cook, stirring occasionally, until venison is pink in color. Mix in tomatoes, vinegar, raisins, salt and pepper. Cook over low flame until liquid is reduced by half. Adjust seasonings and serve with tortillas and fresh salsa. Makes 6 to 8 servings.

Venison Roast

Categories: game

Yield: 4 servings

3 lb chunk of venison roast (or1 roll it if its in steak 1 form)

2 c onion - cut up (2 in. 1 pieces)

2 c potato - cut up

1 c carrots - cut up

1 c fresh mushrooms - sliced

2 tb liquid smoke

3 tb (or more) worchestershire

1 sauce

3 tb (or more) soy sauce

1/2 c beef broth

Put a LARGE oven cooking bag in an oblong baking pan (so that the bag fits inside the pan). To the bag, add the venison. Add all liquids, then veggies around the meat. Put the 'shrooms on top of everything else, then the spices on top of them. You want to have about 1 inch of liquid in the bottom of the bag, so if you need more, add a little water (or white wine!).

Seal bag. Poke several small holes in top of bag to let steam escape. Bake at 300-325 for 3-1/2 hours. (If you chop the veggies big, they won't overcook).

Frank's Sure-Kill Venison Chili

Yield: 1 servings

3 lb venison cubed/course ground

3 cn kidney beans as extender

3 cn tomato sauce

2 cn tomato paste

1 lg onion

1/4 lb butter

1 lb fresh mushrooms

6 garlic wedges

1 cn stewed tomatoes (optional)

1 c barbeque sauce

1/2 c sugar-more or less to taste

1/2 c water

3 tb red pepper

6 jalapeno peppers - diced

3 tb louisiana hot sauce

4 tb worcestershire sauce

2 tb oregeno

1/2 bell pepper-finely chopped

1 other spices that look good

1 that you have a mind to use.

Brown the venison (or other wild game) with some butter. Venison tends to be somewhat dry, so add butter as needed. Drain well. Add to 6-8 quart slow cooker. (A large pot on the stove will work, but overnight cooking is preferred). Add other ingredients, mixing well. Add only enough water to prevent burning. Cook covered for 2 hours at boil. Reduce heat to

~200 degrees and cook until you can't keep everyone away. Consistancy should be fairly thick. Cook uncovered if too thin.

Top with shredded cheese of choice and serve with fresh cornbread. Freezes well if any left over.

Venison Meat Loaf With Chili Sauce

Yield: 6 servings

4 slices fresh bread

1/2 c water

2 lb ground venison

1 medium onion

1 ts salt

1/4 ts pepper

2 eggs

1 c chili sauce

Soften bread in water and add remaining ingredients. Mix well, pack in pan and cover with chili sauce. Bake at 375 degrees F. for 45 minutes.

Tomato Venison Pot Roast

Yield: 6 servings

2 1/2 lb chuck or rump venison

1 tb margarine or butter

2 c tomato juice

1 tb salt

1 clove garlic

4 medium potatoes

6 carrots

Brown meat slowly in margarine or butter. When well browned add tomato juice, salt and garlic. Cover lightly and simmer until tender, about 3 1/2 hours. Add potatoes and carrots about 45 minutes before meat is done.

Elk/Deer Sauerbraten I

Categories: game

Yield: 6 servings

3 lb elk or deer

2 1/2 c vinegar

3 c water

2 medium onions, sliced

1/2 lemon sliced

6 whole cloves

3 bay leaves

6 whole black pepper

1 1/2 ts salt

1 ts fat

1 1/2 tb flour

Place meat in a large bowl; add vinegar, water, onions, cloves, pepper and salt. Let meat stand 48 hours in refrigerator, turning occasionally.

Remove meat, brown in hot fat. Remove meat and add flour, brown and add 2 cups vinegar marinade mixture; cook until mixture thickens. Add meat and simmer for two hours. Remove, slice meat and pour gravy over meat.

Elk/Deer Spanish Pot Roast

Categories: game

Yield: 6 servings

3 lb pot roast of elk or deer

11 sliced stuffed olives

1/4 lb salt pork

1 medium onion, sliced

3 tb margarine or butter

2 c canned tomatoes

1 ts salt

1/4 ts pepper

1 ts sugar

Cut small pockets along sides of the roast with a sharp knife. Fill these pockets with slicedolives and salt pork which has been cut into small strips. Brown onions slices in margarine or butter. Remove onions and blown roast in hot fat. Add canned tomatoes, salt, pepper, sugar and browned onion. Cover and simmer until meat is tender - about 3 to 4 hours. Thicken liquid for gravy.

Leg Roast of Venison

Categories: game

Yield: 6 servings

3 lb leg roast elk or deer

5 slices salt pork

1 onion

1 apple

1 ts salt

1/4 ts pepper

1/4 ts allspice

2 sprigs of rosemary

2 bay leaves

Cut gashes in roast about 2 inches apart and half through the thickness of roast. Place in each gash a slice of salt pork, onion and apple. Top with a few more slices of onion. Sprinkle roast with spices and herbs. Plase meat on a rack in a roasting pan. Bake in 300 degrees F. oven until done, 2 to 4 hours, depending on tenderness of meat. Remove herbs before serving.

Venison With Almonds

Categories: game

Yield: 6 servings

1/2 c crushed pineapple

2 tb margarine or butter

1 1/2 tb cornstarch

1/2 c pineapple juice

2 c meat stock

2 c cooked, cubed elk or deer

1/2 c sliced celery

1/2 c slivered toasted almonds

1 ts salt

Brown pineapple in the margarine or butter for 5 minutes. Mix cornstarch with pineapple juice. Add mixture and meat stock to the browned pineapple. Cook over low heat, stirring constantly, until thickened. Boil 2 minutes, then add meat, celery, almonds and salt. Allow to heat through and serve with rice or chow mein noodles.

Jellied Venison Salad

Categories: game

Yield: 6 servings

1 1/2 tb unflavored gelatin

1/2 c cold water

1 bouillon cube

1 1/2 c boiling water

1/4 c vinegar

1/2 ts salt

2 c cooked, diced, leftover--roast of; venison

2 tb green pepper, chopped

2 tb pimiento, cut in small pieces

4 sweet pickles, chopped

2 tb celery, diced

1 tb onion, diced

2 tb cooked cut green beans

Soak gelatin in cold water. Dissolve bouillon cube and gelatin in boiling water. Add vinegar and salt. Cool this mixture and when just beginning to set add the rest of ingredients. Pour into individual molds or greased

8- inch square baking dish. Chill and serve on a bed of lettuce with mayonnaise.

Hawaiian Venison

Categories: game

Yield: 1 servings

1 lb boneless elk/deer round stk

1/4 c flour

2 tb margarine or butter

1/2 c boiling water

1 ts salt

2 or 3 green peppers

1/2 c pineapple chunks

-SAUCE

2 1/2 tb cornstarch

1/2 c pineapple juice

1/4 c vinegar

1/4 c sugar

1 1/2 tb soy sauce

Cut steak into 1-inch cubes and dredge with flour. Brown meat cubes on all sides in hot fat. Add water and salt. Simmer gently until meat is tender.

Clean green peppers and cut into 1-inch squares. Boil 10 minutes and drain. Add pepper squares and pneapple chunks to browned meat. SAUCE: Combine cornstarch, pineapple juice, vinegar, sugar and soy sauce and cook until sauce is clear and thick. Pour sauce over meat mixture and simmer 5 minutes. Serve over Chinese noodles or cooked rice.

Venison Shortcake

Categories: game

Yield: 6 servings

1 slice bacon, diced

1/4 c sliced onions

1 lb ground elk/deer

1/2 ts salt

1/4 ts pepper

2 tb flour

1 1/4 c water

1/2 ts prepared mustard

1/8 c tomato catsup

----SHORTCAKE---

2 c flour

2 ts baking powder

1/2 ts salt

4 tb shortening

2/3 c milk

1 melted butter or margarine

Saute' bacon and onions until slightly browned. Add meat, salt, pepper, and cook until browned. Add 2 tablespoons flour and blend. Add water, mustard, and catsup. Bring to a brisk boil, stirring constantly.

For shortcake, sift flour, baking powder and salt together twice. Cut in shortening. Add milk gradually, mixing to soft dough. Turn out on and knead slightly. Roll 1/4-inch thick and cut with floured 3-inch biscuit cutter. Place half the biscuits on baking sheets, brush with melted butter and place remaining biscuits on top. Bake in hot oven (425 degees F.) 12 to 15 minutes. To serve split shortcakes and pile meat mixture between halves.

Venison Barbecue

Categories: game, barbeque

Yield: 6 servings

3 lb venison roast

1 c catsup

1 tb salt

2 tb worcestershire sauce

1/4 c vinegar

1 tb butter

1/8 ts cinnamon

3 slices lemon

1 onion, sliced thin

1/8 ts allspice

Sear 3-pound roast of venison in frying pan. Mix remaining ingredients in saucepan and bring mixture to boil, stirring to avoid burning, and simmer 10 minutes. Cover venison with the sauce and roast in moderate oven (350 degrees F.). Cook 1 1/2 to 2 hours - turning occasionally.

Curried Venison

Yield: 6 servings

1 1/2 md onion, minced

3 stalks celery, chopped

2 apples, minced

1/4 c salad oil or shortening

2 ts curry powder

1 ts salt

1/8 ts pepper

1/4 ts ginger

1/4 ts tabasco sauce

1/2 tb worcestershire sauce

2 c stock or bouillon

1/8 c flour

2 lb cooked elk or deer, cubed

1 c cream or canned milk

1 egg yolk, well beaten

3 c boiled rice

Saute' onions, celery and apples in oil until slightly brown. Stir in curry powder and simmer 5 minutes. Add remaining seasonings and stock and cook 20 minutes. Stir in flour mixed with water and cook 5 minutes, stirring until thickened. Remove from heat and allow to stand one hour. Reheat and add cooked meat, cream or milk, and egg yolk just before serving. Heat to boiling point, stirring constantly. Serve over rice.

Venison Roll-Ups

Categories: game

Yield: 6 servings

2 lb round steak (elk or deer)

1 salt

1 pepper

1/2 lb pork sausage

4 medium-sized carrots

1 flour

1 shortening

Pound thinly cut steak with saucer edge or meat hammer. Cut into 4- inch sqares. Sprinkle with salt and pepper and spread with sausage meat. Peel carrots and quarter lengthwise. Place several strips on each piece of meat. Roll and tie with string or fasten with toothpicks or skewers. Flour lightly, Brown in hot shortening. Partly cover with water, cover pan, and cook in moderate oven (359 degrees F) until tender - 1-1/2 to 2 hours.

Stuffed Steaks

Categories: game

Yield: 4 servings

1 1/2 slices day old bread

1/2 ts salt

2 ts green pepper, finely chopped

2 ts onions, minced

2 ts celery, finely chopped

1 salt

1 flour

2 club steaks,

1 thick, elk-or deer

2 tb margarine or butter

1/2 c water

Make a dressing by combining bread, broken in small pieces, 1/2 teaspoon salt, green pepper, onion and celery. Salt steaks and dredge with flour.

Cut slits halfway through steaks and fill with dressing. Using a pressure pan, brown steaks in margarine or butter. Add 1/2 cup of water and cook at 10 psi about 20 minutes.

Creamed Venison

Categories: game

Yield: 2 servings

1 lb cubed elk/deer round steak

3 tb margarine or butter

2 c medium white sauce

1 ts celery salt

1/4 ts pepper

3 tb chopped parsley

2 ts worcestershire sauce

1/4 c pickle relish

----TOPPING

1/2 c dry bread crumbs 2 tb margarine or butter

Brown steak in 3 tablespoons margarine or butter. Add a small amount of water and cook in a covered skillet until tender, adding a little water from time to time as needed. When done add white sauce, seasonings, parsley and pickle relish. Put mixture in a greased casserole. Sprinkle top with bread crumbs and dot with margarine or butter. Bake in a moderate oven (350 degrees F.) until crumbs are browned. onions, apple and butter with all other stuffing ingredients, and brown quickly in remaining butter. Place rabbit in a casserole, stuff, surround with excess stuffing, add well-seasoned stock, and cook for 1 3/4 hours, or until tender, at 350 degrees.

Deer Filet A'tournedos Brennan

Categories: game

Yield: 1 servings

4 deer filets of loin

2 tb butter

1 tb flour

1/2 c mushroom juice

1/4 c wine, red

1/4 ts worcestershire sauce

1/4 ts salt

1 pepper, black, dash

1 tomato, ripe large

1/2 c mushrooms, sliced

In a small saucepan melt butter and saute mushrooms. Add flour and cook slowly a few minutes until slightly browned. Stir in wine, juice and seasonings. Cook until thickened.

Meanwhile, season and grill filets to taste, rare or medium rare. Cut the tomato into four slices and grill. Arrange tomato slice on each filet and pour over mushroom sauce.

USE large amount of charcoal, almost 2 layers, for rapid grilling. Hugg's Note: Add whole hickory nuts or pecans, in husks, to the grill to make an aromatic smoke. Won't flame before done.

Venison Jerky

Categories: game

Yield: 10 servings

2 lb sliced venison

1/8 thick

2 tb worcestershire sauce

2 tb soy sauce

1 tb salt

1 ts ground red pepper

2 cloves garlic, sliced

1 c corn whiskey

1 c water

Slice the meat when it is lightly frozen. The cuts should be long, thin and with the grain. Cut across the grain if you want more tender, but more brittle jerky.

Trim off all of the fat. Marinate strips in a glass container overnight. You may substitute 2 cups of red wine for the corn whiskey and water.

Pat dry and arrange pieces side by side on an oven roasting rack, with- out overlap. Cook at minimum heat (150F) for 6 hours. Leave oven door ajar to allow moisture to escape. Meat should be dark, dry and store jerky in a cool, airtight container.

Deer Jerky Marinade

Categories: game, sauces

Yield: 1 servings

3 lb deer meat, thinly sliced

3/4 c wine, dry

1/3 c lemon juice

1/4 c onion, minced

1/4 c brown sugar

2 ts liquid smoke

1 ts seasoned salt

1/4 ts pepper

3 ea bay leaves

Marinade deer meat for 24 hours in the marinade mixture, covered, in a cold part of the refrigerator. Turn meat several times. Remove meat, spreading out to bring to room temp. Place on greased racks in a smoker and smoke at a low heat (160-190 degrees) for 5 to 7 hours, until meat becomes slightly translucent and darkly red, near black. Store in plastic bags in refrigerator.

Sugar Cured Venison Jerky

Categories: game

Yield: 1 servings

5 lb venison roast

1 1/2 c sugar

1 ts brown sugar

15 ts salt

1 oz liquid smoke

2 ts garlic

3 ts seasoning salt

1 ts black pepper

Serves several people.

Cut venison 1 to 2 inches wide and 1/4-inch thick, 6 to 10 inches long. Put in large mixing bowl and add sugar a little at a time. Be sure to mix well. Mix brown sugar and all other spices and mix all together. Put in refrigerator approximately 6 to 8 hours. Take out and put in oven on racks, lightly pepper. Cook at a maximum of 150F until completely dry, approximately 8 hours.

Smoked Spicy Venison Jerky

Categories: game

Yield: 1 servings

4 lb venison roast

1/2 c brown sugar

1/4 c salt

1 c water

1 c red wine

1/2 ts onion powder

1/2 ts pepper

1/2 ts garlic powder

1/2 ts tabasco sauce

Serves many people.

Trim fat from venison and cut into 1/4- to 1/2-inch thick slices. Place meat into the marinade made by combining the above ingredients in a glass or ceramic bowl. Marinate at least 8 hours in a cool place. Remove to a rack and allow to air dry until they become glazed. Do not rinse. Smoke for

12 to 16 hours depending on degree of desired dryness. Use approximately 3 panfuls of hickory or cherry wood chips to add to flavor.

Venison Sauces

Categories: game, sauces, scottish

Yield: 6 servings

1/4 lb sugar

1/2 pt champagne vinegar

1 sweet sauce:

6 oz white or red currant jelly

6 oz white or red wine

Sharp Sauce:

Sharp Sauce:--A quarter-pound of the best loaf-sugar, or white candy-sugar, dissolved in a half-pint of Champagne vinegar, and carefully skimmed.

Sweet Sauce:--Melt some white or red currant jelly with a glass of white or red wine, whichever suits best in color; or serve jelly unmelted in a small sweetmeat-glass. This sauce answers well for hare, fawn, or kid, and for roast mutton to many tastes.

Gravy for Venison:--Make a pint of gravy of trimmings of venison or shanks of mutton thus: broil the meat on a quick fire till it is browned, then stew it slowly. Skim, strain, and serve the gravy it yields, adding salt and a teaspoonful of walnut pickle.

Heat to boiling, stirring occasionally, reduce heat and cover. Simmer until wild rice is tender, 40 to 50 minutes. Stir in pine nuts, pears and currants.

Venison Chili

Categories: mexican, game, chili, spices

Yield: 3 servings

3 tb vegetable oil

1 lg onion, finely chopped

2 cloves garlic, minced

1 pequin chile, minced

1 1/4 lb venison, cubed 1/2

3/4 lb ground venison

28 oz can of crushed tomatoes

3 tb red wine vinegar

3 tb ground chili powder

2 tb ground cumin

2 tb worcestershire sauce

1/2 ts cayenne pepper

1 green bell pepper, chopped

2 ts salt

1 fresh ground black pepper

10 oz red kidney beans, drained

3 tb masa harina *

* Mixed with a little water into a smooth paste for thickening chili.

Venison Loaf With Noodles

Categories: game

Yield: 1 servings

--VENISON LOAF--

1 1/2 lb venison, ground

3/4 c milk

1 pk lipton's onion soup mix

1 egg, lightly beaten

1 1/2 c bread crumbs (soft)

1/4 c catsup

1 tb brown sugar

1 tb prepared mustard (coleman's)

4 sl jack cheese

----POPPY SEED NOODLES----

1/2 lb egg noodles (3 cups), -uncooked

2 tb butter

1/2 c half-and-half

1/2 c jack cheese, grated

1 ts poppy seeds

VENISON LOAF: Lightly oil a 9-inch ring mold. Combine milk, onion soup mix, egg and bread crumbs. Let stand until mixture is mushy. Combine mixture with ground venison. Shape into mold and turn out onto baking pan. (You can do this with any meatloaf: very pretty and easy to slice).

Combine the catsup, brown sugar and prepared mustard. Brush mixture onto loaf. Bake in a preheated 400-degree oven for 40 minutes, brushing with catsup mixture once more during baking.

Remove loaf from oven and arrange Jack cheese slices over loaf. Bake about 5 minutes longer until cheese melts. Slide onto serving plate. Fill center with Poppy Seed Noodles. POPPY SEED NOODLES: Cook the noodles according to directions on the package, or until tender. Drain well. Toss with butter, half-and-half and Jack cheese. Sprinkle on the poppy seeds and toss well to mix.

Venison Meat Loaf

Categories: game

Yield: 1 servings

3/4 lb venison, ground

1/4 lb sausage, ground

1 egg

2 tb parsley, chopped

1 tb butter, softened

1 tb bread crumbs

1 ts lemon juice

1 ts salt

1/4 ts pepper

1 tb onion flakes, dried

1 c water

1/2 pk lipton's onion soup mix

Combine all ingredients except the Onion Soup Mix and the cup of water and shape into a loaf. Place in a lightly greased pan.

Bake 1 hour 350-degrees. Baste every 10 minutes with a combination of 1 cup water and 1/2 package dried onion soup mix.

Venison Meatballs

Categories: game

Yield: 1 servings

1 1/2 lb venison, ground

2 c sour cream, divided

2 tb catsup

1 1/4 ts salt

1/4 ts pepper

1/2 ts garlic salt

1/2 ts oregano

1 tb oil

1 tb water

2 ts dill weed paprika

Combine venison, 1/4 cup sour cream, catsup, salt, pepper, garlic salt and oregano. Shape into meatballs the size of walnuts.

Brown meatballs in hot oil. Pour off any excess oil. Add water, cover and simmer 15 minutes. Remove meatballs to your serving dish.

Combine remaining sour cream, salt and dill in skillet in which meatballs were cooked. Heat through and pour over meatballs. Sprinkle with paprika.

Serve with rice or noodles.

This will serve 6 for dinner or more as appetizers.

Deer Jerky Mcdermott

Categories: game

Yield: 1 servings

1 deer, sliced 1/8 thick

2 tb hickory smoked salt

1 tb garlic salt

2 tb monosodium glutamate

4 tb seasoned pepper

2/3 c soy sauce

1/3 c worcester sauce smoked

1 tabasco sauce to taste

Sprinkle meat with dry mixture, both sides. Drape on oven racks without touching while oven heats to 200 degrees. Place in oven with door open 2-3 inches. After one hour, baste with sauce, repeating every half-hour for the remaining two hours at 200 degrees. Now drop oven to 170 degrees and finish meat in 45 to 90 minutes.

Magnum Deer Chili

Categories: game

Yield: 1 servings

2 lb deer, or other game, ground

40 oz red kidney beans, can

46 oz v-8 juice, can

3 oz jalapeno peppers

1 tb sugar

1 tb chili powder

1 tb cumin

1 1/2 tb onion, dry, minced

1/2 tb garlic salt

1/2 tb red pepper

Brown meat in a black iron pot over medium-high heat. Drain jalapeno and chop. Drain kidney brans, rinse with cold water and drain again. After meat is brown, add all other ingredients and cook over medium heat for 4 hours. Add additional cumin, chili powder and red pepper to taste. Use caution with red pepper- it is easier to heat up with pepper than to cool off!

Marinaded Deer Roast

Categories: game

Yield: 1 servings

8 lb deer roast (ham)

1/2 lb salt pork, cut in strips

1 c currant jelly

4 tb flour

1 tb brandy

4 c vinegar

4 c water

1 tb salt

1 tb red pepper

1 tb pepper, black

3 ea garlic clove, minced

3 ea bay leaves

1 ts cloves

1 ts allspice

1 ts thyme

Mix all ingredients after brandy into marinade. Pour over roast and soak for at least 6-8 hours, turning several times. Before roasting punch several holes in the roast with a sharp knife. Insert salt pork with additional garlic, cloves. Cook at 325-350 degrees for 20-25 minutes per pound. Baste frequently with drippings and marinade. When tender, remove meat and keep warm while making gravy. GRAVY: In the roasting pan slowly melt 1 C currant jelly with drippings and marinade. Add flour mixed with water to thicken. When gravy is desired consistency, add 1 Tbsp brandy, stir well and serve.

Suggestions: Use muscadine jelly for better tasting gravy.

Venison Benison

Categories: game

Yield: 1 servings

1 ea deer fillet, med size

2 tb butter, melted

1 tb flour

2 tb orange juice

1 ea bay leaf

1/2 lb mushrooms, chopped

2 tb butter, cold

1 salt & pepper to taste

Mix melted butter with chopped mushrooms and cook for about five minutes. Stir, add flour and brown. Add orange juice, salt and pepper and bay leaf.

Cover and simmer until sauce is creamy. Rub fillet with 2 Tbsp solid butter, sprinkle with pepper. Broil over very hot coals for 5 minutes per side. Place in a hot broiling plate, sprinkle with salt, add mushroom-orange juice sauce and cook until done to your desire, basting while it cooks.

Use 2 levels of charcoal briquets for hot fire.

Add hickory nuts or pecans, whole in husks, for smoke flavor.

Smoked Deer Ham I

Categories: game

Yield: 1 servings

1 ea deer ham, 8-10 lb

3 tb red pepper

1/2 c salt

1/4 c vinegar

4 tb pepper, black

Wash ham carefully and trim away fat or cartilage. Make small slits in meat with sharpe knife about 2 in. apart and 1 in. deep, all over the roast.

Make a paste of the ingredients and stuff each cut slit with a small teaspoon of seasoning paste. Rub remaining seasoning over outside of roast.

Seal tight in a container and refrigerate for 24 - 48 hours, turning over 2 or 3 times. When ready to cook, place on spit over coals and smoke approximately 4 - 5 hours. When done, wrap in foil and keep very warm till serving.

Hugg's Note: Electric skillet with hickory nut hulls make excellent smoke generating stuff. Also green maple, bay.

Deer Sausage I

Categories: game

Yield: 1 servings

10 lb deer meat, lean

10 lb pork, fresh, lean

3 oz water

1 oz pepper, black

3/4 oz ginger, ground

1 1/4 oz nutmeg

1/2 oz allspice

1/2 oz paprika

2 ts garlic powder

12 oz salt

1/2 lb dried milk

2 1/2 ts liquid smoke

Grind together the two meats, mix thoroughly. Add measured water. Mix spices thoroughly and mix well into meat mixture. If sausage is to be smoked, omit the liquid smoke. You may stuff sausage into casings, making 6-8" links, or make into patties for freezing. To cook, place in a frying pan with a cover, adding water to the 1/3 mark on the sausage. Boil for 15 minutes covered, then remove. Drain most of the fat from the pan; replace sausage and brown. Make gravy in pan after sausage done.

Venison Ragout With Onions

Categories: game

Yield: 1 servings

2 lb deer neck and shank

24 ea pearl onions

1 1/2 ea onion, chopped

1 lb fresh mushrooms, chopped

1 tb tomato sauce

3 tb wine, sherry or port

2 c beef stock

2 c wine, dry red

3 tb flour

1/4 ts salt

2 tb butter

Cut meat from bones into chunks about 3/4". Heat 1/4 stick of butter in a large steel or aluminum pot. Add 1 tsp olive oil to retard burning. Brown deer chunks until well-seared, then add sherry or port and cook for 10 minutes more. Remove from pot and set aside. To the liquid remaining in the pan add pearl or chopped onion and brown until golden. Add tomato paste, stirring in well. Add flour and stir into mixture. Return deer to pot, adding stock. Add 1/3 the red wine, bring to a boil, then simmer for 3 hours or until tender, adding wine by 1/3 until used up. Add mushrooms 30 minutes before serving. Serve over buttered noodles or rice.

Suggestions: Leave out mushrooms and substitute chopped carrots at start.

Deer And Barley Soup

Categories: soups, game

Yield: 1 servings

2 ea deer shanks (or equal)

1 c barley, pearl

1 c peas, green split

2 ea onions, chopped

2 ea garlic clove, finely chopped

1 ea bell pepper, seeded, chopped

14 c beef or chicken stock

4 tb butter

1 tb salt

1/4 ts pepper

Brown garlic, onion and pepper in butter. Add deer, cut into 1" pieces, and brown lightly. Add stock and remaining ingredients and bring to a boil.

Cover and simmer for 2-3 hours, until meat is tender. Season according to taste.

Shank took 3 hours to become tender.

Deer Sausage Peperone

Categories: game

Yield: 1 servings

5 lb deer, ground

5 lb pork butt, ground

1 lb pork fat, ground

2 1/2 oz sausage seasoning

SEASONING: Dan-Dee Seasoning Metairie Louisiana Mix ground meats with seasoning and form into patties 3" in diameter, 3/8 " to 1/2 " thick. Place patties on squares of waxed paper, four high, and place six squares in a plastic zip-loc bag and freeze. Recipe makes 78 patties when 5-5-1 pounds of meat used.

IMPROVE by using smoked sow belly (Kroger, bacon department) instead of fat pork, This gives smoked flavor to sausage.

Makes a very lean sausage which needs water to cook.

Deer Soup Stock

Categories: soups, game

Yield: 1 servings

2 ea deer bones, cracked, large

1/8 ts nutmeg

1/16 ts mace

12 ea peppercorns, green, crushed

8 c water

1/4 ts smoked salt

Crack deer bones after removing from meat (large ham bone & pelvic bones, etc). Place in large stew pot, add seasonings. Bring to a boil, then cover and simmer for three hours. Strain stock through tea strainer, then through cloth to remove any particles. Allow to cool, then skim off any fat which accumulates. Use as base for soup or stew.

Charlie's Deer Stew

Categories: game

Yield: 1 servings

3 ea venison (to 4 lb)

1 flour

3 tb bacon fat

1 1/2 c hot water

1 c wine, dry red

1 ts mixed thyme, basil, marjoram

1 ts dried parsley

1 ea onion, large

1 1/2 ts salt

1/2 ts coarse red pepper

3 ea carrots, scraped/quartered

3 ea potatoes, scraped/quartered

Remove sinews and bones from deer; cut meat into bite sized pieces & roll in flour. Brown in bacon fat, wine, herbs, onions, salt and pepper. Cover pot and and bring to a boil. Lower heat and simmer two hours. Add carrots & potatoes. Cover and simmer 1 hour, adding more hot water if needed. When meat is tender and vegetables done, serve hot with french bread.

Venison Ham

Categories: game

Yield: 1 servings

2 tb flour

2 tb vegetable oil

3 c water, hot

2 ea onions, large, chop coarse

9 oz mustard pickles

3 tb vinegar

3 tb pancake syrup

4 tb worcestershire sauce

12 oz chili sauce

1 cayenne pepper (to taste)

1 salt & pepper to taste

1 ea deer ham, large

Combine flour and oil and cook over medium heat, stirring constantly, to make a roux. Add hot water gradually, stirring to blend. Place ham in roasting pan. Surround roast with onions, sprinkling some over top. Salt and pepper liberally. Pour roux over roast. Cover pan and bake one hour at

350 degrees. Make a sauce with remaining ingredients. Pour sauce over roast and bake three more hours, uncovered for the last hour. Slice and serve with gravy over rice.

Suggestions: To decrease wild taste of deer, marinate in buttermilk overnight,

Herb Marinaded Deer Roast

Categories: game

Yield: 1 servings

1 ea deer roast

4 tb peanut oil

1 ea onion, chopped

2 ea garlic clove, minced

4 tb flour

1 c beef broth

1 ea tomato, peeled and chopped

1 ts thyme

1 ts tarragon

1 salt & pepper to taste

Cook deer over hot charcoal for 3-4 hours, basting often with the marinade, but reserving one cup for the sauce. Heat oil in a pan and add onion and garlic. Saute for 5 minutes and sprinkle on flour. Cook and stir over moderate heat for 15 minutes or until flour is brown. Stir in the broth and reserved cup of marinade and bring to a boil. Reduce heat. Add tomato and herbs. Simmer one hour. Correct seasonings. Serve with meat.

Boiled Deer Ardennes

Categories: game

Yield: 1 servings

2 lb deer, lean

4 tb flour

1 c brown vinegar

1 c water, cold

1 ea onion, small, chop fine

1/4 ts cloves, ground

1/2 ts ginger, ground

1/2 ts salt

1/8 ts pepper, black

Cut deer into bite-size pieces. Boil chunks of deer in water seasoned well with salt and pepper. Remove and drain well. While boiling deer, make a gravy: Mix 4 Tbsp flour with cold water to make a thin paste. Place in saucepan or frying pan. Add all other ingredients, stirring well over medium heat until a smooth gravy is formed. Pour gravy over deer chunks immediately before serving. Time it and take great care that all is piping hot.

VARIATION: Boil deer in seasoned broth by adding a small amount of any popular marinade or herb/seafood seasoning.

Deer Sausage II

Categories: game

Yield: 1 servings

2 lb bacon, smoked, unsliced

5 lb deer meat, lean

1 tb sage, rubbed

1 tb smoked salt

Grind meats, blending together thoroughly with salt and sage. Smoke in links or cook in patties in a pan.

Barbequed Deer Ribs I

Categories: game

Yield: 1 servings

1 c catsup

1/4 c vinegar

1/4 c worcestershire sauce

1 ts salt

1 ts pepper, black

2 ts chili powder

1/4 ts cayenne pepper

2 ea onions, finely chopped

1 1/2 c water

Split washed ribs into spareribs. Cover with sauce, cover the pan and bake in a moderate oven (350) for an hour. Uncover and continue to bake for another 30 minutes. Turn during last half-hour several times, to brown. You pick your favorite barbeque sauce.

Boiled Deer Tongue

Categories: game

Yield: 1 servings

1 ea deer tongue

1 tb salt

4 ea peppers, whole

3 ea bay leaves

2 ea cloves, whole

Use ingredients above for one deer tongue, and add equal increase for each added tongue to cook. Wash the tongue(s) well and cover with water in a pot. Add spices and salt and simmer covered until tender. Remove from the water and peel off the outer covering, which is a modified 'skin' of sensory cells.

Serve hot or cold with any of the myriad deer sauces listed here. You may spice it up to suit yourself during cooking.

Deer Sauce I

Categories: game, sauces

Yield: 1 servings

1/2 c jelly, currant or grape

4 tb butter

1/2 ts dried herbs

Melt and blend in a sauce panserving in a gravy boat for individual use. Pick your favorite herbs, usually aromatic ones such as sage, cloves or allspice.

Suggestions: USE muscadine jelly, a perfect taste to compliment deer.

Deer Sauce II

Categories: game, sauces

Yield: 1 servings

1/4 c marinade, strained

1 c jelly, strained

1 tb lemon juice

1 ea ginger, powdered, pinch

2 tb whiskey, scotch/bourbon

Heat and blend thoroughly in a small sauce pan. Serve in a preheated gravy boat for individual use.

Note: Muscadine jelly is the very best with deer.

Deer Marinade I

Categories: game, sauces

Yield: 1 servings

2 c wine, claret or other red

2 c vinegar

1 ts worcestershire sauce

1 ea bay leaf

2 ea cloves, whole

1 salt, pinch

4 cups of either wine or vinegar may be used in place of the combination. Marinade as short as two hours or up to 48 hours, depending on how you judge the tenderness and tastiness of your game. Save the marinade and use again or add to gravies and soups (sparingly). Note: Hunt TROPHIES

FOR THE POT (Spikes & Forkhorns). ADJUSTMENT: 12 crushed green peppercorns and a few black.

Deer Marinade II

Categories: game, sauces

Yield: 1 servings

2 c wine, dry

2 c vinegar, white

6 ea bay leaves

12 ea cloves, whole

1 tb peppercorns, black, whole

1 ea onion, large, sliced

Combine ingredients and place meat in a bowl. Pour marinade over meat and cover for from 2 hours to 48 hours (refrigerate if cooking is not planned same day). Turn meat several times. Save marinade as basting sauce, repeat use, gravy flavoring or soup additive. You should judge meat tenderness and flavor to decide how long to marinade. Hugg's Note: If meat is badly bloodied, add 2 Tbsp salt and increase vinegar by 1 C.

Deer Marinade III

Categories: game, sauces

Yield: 1 servings

1 ea lemon, juice of

1/2 c vinegar, wine

1/4 ts tarragon

2 ea onions, sliced

1 ts chili powder

1/2 c water

2 ts salt

2 ea bay leaves

1/4 ts pepper, black

1/2 c tomato catsup

1 ea garlic clove, crushed

Mix ingredients in a large bowl. Place meat therein and turn several times. Cover. Marinade for from 2 hours to 48 hours, dependent upon your assessment of tenderness and flavor. Save marinade for soups, gravies, or later use with another meat. Hugg's Note: The use of chili powder is questionable (unless you are a Texan, when it becomes basic.

Deer Marinade IV

Categories: game, sauces

Yield: 1 servings

1 ea wine, dry white, bottle

1 c vinegar

1/2 c oil, any type

1 ea onion, large, sliced

2 ea carrots, large, sliced thin

4 ea shallots, chopped

3 ea parsley, chopped, sprigs

1 ts salt

6 ea peppercorns, crushed

4 ea juniper berries

1/4 ts thyme

Place cutup and chopped vegetables around meat in a large bowl. Pour mixed liquids over it. Oil rises to the top and retains flavor of marinade. Use for 2 hours to 48 hours, dependent on how you assess the tenderness and flavor of the meat. Retain marinade liquid for soup base, gravies or reuse later. Keep meat in refrigerator if not cooking the same day. OPTIONS: Omit juniper berries. Add rosemary or tarragon with or in place of thyme.

Deer Marinade V

Categories: game, sauces

Yield: 1 servings

1 lb carrots, raw

1 lb onions, yellow

1/2 lb celery, incl. tops

8 c vinegar

4 c wine, red

1 tb parsley, chopped

3 ea bay leaves

1 ts thyme

1 ts peppercorns, crushed

1 tb allspice, whole

1 ts salt

Saute carrots, onions and celery, finely chopped, in 4 Tbsp fat. Don't cook so hot that vegetables become browned. Add remaining ingredients and boil then simmer, covered, for 1/2 hour. Allow to cool and you are ready to use. Cover the meat completely if possible. If not, turn every 1/2 hour while in marinade. Otherwise, if meat fully covered, turn about every 3 hours. Keep meat in marinade for from 2 hours to 48 hours depending on your assessment of the tenderness and flavor of the deer. Refrigerate if more than 8 hours.

Keep marinade, strained, for gravy or soup flavoring.

Big Buck Steak I

Categories: game

Yield: 1 servings

1 ea round steak, 1-1/2 to 2 in.

6 tb flour

1 cn mushroom soup

1 salt & pepper to taste

2 tb frying fat

If you kill a big buck and know he will not be as tender as my spikehorns, cut a round steak about 2 inches thick, dredge in flour, let stand for an hour and then reflour the wet spots. Sear on both sides in a hot, lightly-greased skillet or black iron pot. Now pour the can of soup directly onto the center of the steak, then add enough hot water to cover the meat. Cover the pot or skillet, cook in a moderate (375) oven for about 2 hours or until tender. Suggestions: TRY adding cutup turnips and fresh green beans around the meat, just before pouring the mushroom soup on.

Big Buck Steak II

Categories: game

Yield: 1 servings

1 ea round steak, 1-1/2 to 2 in.

1 marinade, selected

1 tb garlic butter

1 ea onion, finely chopped

1/2 ts flour

2 tb catsup

2 tb olive oil

4 tb water

1 salt & pepper to taste

1 paprika to taste

Dry the marinaded steak and brush with melted garlic butter. Add salt and pepper. Sear on both sides in a little bacon fat, in a black iron pot. Add remaining ingredients and cover, cooking over moderate heat for an hour and a half or until tender. If water cooks down, add wine to replace. Full range of modification to this recipe include tomato sauce instead of catsup, more or different seasonings, added vegetables to cook. Spicier includes bay leaf, clove of garlic, dash of rosemary, thyme, basil or sage. Note: Use hickory smoked salt instead of regular.

Fried Deer Heart

Categories: game

Yield: 1 servings

1 ea deer heart per person

6 tb flour

8 tb cracker crumbs

1/2 c milk

2 tb bacon fat or oil

1 salt & pepper to taste

Slice deer heart thin, add salt and pepper. Roll in flour, dip in milk, and roll in cracker crumbs, and fry on both sides to golden brown. Eat now or add broth and simmer for 3 to 5 minutes. Drain and serve hot. Hearts can be washed and marinaded if desired.

Deer Heart And Kidney Stew

Categories: game

Yield: 1 servings

1 heart and kidneys from deer

1 ea onion, minced

1 cn mushroom soup

1 c wine, red

4 c water

1 tb butter or margarine

1 salt & pepper to taste

1 noodles, rice, saffron rice

Boil heart and kidneys in lightly salted water to cover until tender. Cool and slice into bite-sized pieces. Saute onion in butter until transparent. Add remaining ingredients, including 1 cup of broth in which meat is boiled. Allow to simmer for about 15 minutes more. Serve over noodles or rice. Wild rice is also excellent with this.

Venison Swiss Steak

Categories: main dish, meats, game

Yield: 4 servings

4 venison steaks

1/2 lb each

1/3 c flour

1/4 ts pepper

1/8 ts seasoned salt

4 tb cooking oil

1/2 c minced onion

6 fresh sliced mushrooms

1 beef bouillon cube

Mix dry ingredients and dredge each steak. Heat cooking oil over medium heat in a heavy frying pan and brown steaks. When steaks are turned onion, mushrooms and brown. Add 2-1/2 cups water and bouillion cube, cover and simmer for one hour or until a fork can easily be withdrawn from meat. Misture can be thickened to desired consistency with remaining flour mixture.

Serve over hot buttered noodles, potatoes, bread or toast.

Hungryman's Stew With Venison

Yield: 6 servings

3 lb venison

2 onions, chopped

3 tb worchestershire sauce

2 lb potatoes

1 cn green beans

1 cn wax beans

1 cn corn

1 lb carrots, sliced

2 qt water

2 ts seasoned salt

1 ts pepper

2 ts oregano

2 ts garlic powder

4 tb cornstarch

Cut venison into chunks. In a large stew pot, lightly brown venison with chopped onions and Worchestershire Sauce. Cut potatoes into cubes. Add potatoes, green beans, wax beans, corn, carrots, water, seasoned salt, pepper, oregano, and garlic powder.

Bring mixture to a boil, then turn down to simmer. Stir often. Simmer 2 1/2 to 3 hours. For last 1/2 hour, take some juice from the stew pot, and add cornstarch. Stir until dissolved. Add back into mixture.

Crock Pot Venison Stew

Categories: game

Yield: 6 servings

2 lb venison cubes

2 tb oil

3 stalks celery, diced

1/2 c chopped onion

2 cloves garlic, minced

1 tb parsley, chopped

1/2 c water

1/2 c dry red wine

1 c tomato sauce

1 salt and pepper to taste

1 oregano

1 basil

Brown meat in oil. Place celery and onion at the bottom of the crock pot. Add browned meat and remaining ingredients. Cook on low for 7-10 hours.

Country Style Venison Stew

Categories: game

Yield: 6 servings

1/2 lb bacon or salt pork

2 lb venison steak

4 tb flour

6 c water or beef stock

1 lg tomato, chopped

2 md carrots, sliced

2 md stalks celery, sliced

2 md potatoes, in 1 cubes

1 dozen small white onions

1 tb chopped parsley

1 c fresh green peas

1 salt and pepper to taste

Cut bacon into 1" cubes and saute in large saucepan until lightly browned. Remove and set aside.

Cut venison into 1 1/2 or 2" pieces and brown over high heat in 4 T bacon drippings. Stir in flour. Lower heat and let brown 2-3 minutes, stirring several times. Add liquid and let it simmer 1 hour or more until venison begins to get tender, add more liquid as necessary.

Add all the other ingredients, except peas, and continue to simmer to make a thick stew. Simmer peas in a separate pan until done. Strain and spoon over or around stew when served. Great accompanied by buttered corn muffins and a salad.

Venison Steaks In Wine

Categories: game

Yield: 2 servings

2 sm venison steaks

1 tb butter

1 dash of fennel

1 garlic salt

1 basil

1 white cooking wine

Melt butter in frying pan over medium heat. Put steaks in pan and add fennel, garlic salt and basil. Cook for 5 to 10 minutes or until done to your liking.

Barbecue Venison Chops

Categories: game, barbeque

Yield: 4 servings

20 venison chops

6 oz beer

1 lg onion, chopped

4 pats of butter

2 oz garlic

Place aluminum foil on hot grill with sides folded up, so there is no runoff of juices. Place chops on foil. Add beer, chopped onion and butter. Sprinkle garlic salt on chops each time you turn them. When chops are done, remove foil from grill. Place chops back on grill and sprinkle with garlic salt each time you turn them until charcoal black.

Crock Pot Venison Barbecue

Categories: game, barbeque

Yield: 7 servings

3 lb venison stew meat

1 c onion, diced

4 garlic cloves, chopped

1 c red wine vinegar

1/2 c worcestershire sauce

2 ts lawrey's natural choice

1 seasoning for meat

2 ts seasoned salt

1 lb seasoned bacon

2 c catsup

1/2 c molasses

1/2 c brown sugar

Place venison, onion, garlic, vinegar, Worcestershire sauce and seasoning in crock pot. Cook on high for 1 to 2 hours until meat is cooked. Cook bacon and crumble or chop. Add bacon, catsup, molasses and brown sugar. Turn crock pot on low and heat for the rest of the day. Serve over rice potatoes or toast. NOTE: Venison can be substituted with any red meat, just cut in 1-inch cubes.

Venison And 4-Beans

Categories: game

Yield: 5 servings

2 lb venison

1 lb bacon

1 cn pork and beans

1 cn lima beans

1 cn kidney beans

1 cn navy beans

1/2 onion, cut up

1 green pepper, cut up

1 c mustard

1 c catsup

1 ts brown sugar

1 ts salt

1 ts pepper

Brown venison and bacon. Put all ingredients in crock pot and crook for 4 hours on high temperature setting.

Venison Pizza

Categories: game

Yield: 7 servings

1 lb ground venison

6 c unbleached flour

1 1/2 c buttermilk

4 tb butter or margarine

4 tb honey

1/2 ts salt

1 package of yeast

1/4 c warm water

3 c grated cheese

1 sm onion, chopped

2 cn pizza sauce

1 chives (optional)

1 oregano

1 garlic powder

1 pepper

1 thyme

First, measure flour into large bowl. In a separate container combine buttermilk, butter, honey and salt. Heat the buttermilk mixture to lukewarm. Dissolve yeast in warm water. Add yeast and milk mixture to flour and combine to make a firm dough. Turn dough out and kneed for about 6 minutes, or until it is smooth and elastic. Put the dough in a greased bowl, cover and let rise until double in bulk, about 1 hour. While dough is rising, prepare the toppings. Grate plenty of cheese.

Chop some onions and some wild chive if you have some handy. Fry venison, crumbling it as you fry. When dough has risen, punch it down, divide it in half, and roll out the two parts to fit your baking sheets. The dough should be about 1/4-inch thick. Let the rolled out dough rise for about 15 minutes. Spread a generous amount of pizza sauce on the dough. Sprinkle on plenty of oregano, garlic powder, pepper and a little thyme. Top with grated cheese and the crumbled venison. Bake at 350F for 20 to 30 minutes.

Venison-Beef Stew

Yield: 5 servings

1 lb venison

1 lb beef

1 adolph's meat tenderizer

1 water

2 7. 6 oz. cans stew starter

4 carrots, chopped

1 8. 5 oz. can sweet peas

1 md onion, diced

5 md potatoes, diced

4 celery stalks, chopped

4 tb butter

2 beef bouillon cubes

1 bay leaf

2 ts kitchen bouquet

1 garlic clove, minced

1 ts worcestershire sauce

Cut up venison and beef into bite size pieces. Sprinkle with Adolph's meat tenderizer. Let set for 10 minutes; then brown meat. Add water and rest of ingredients and bring to a boil. Reduce heat, cover and simmer for 1 1/2 hours or until meat and vegetables are tender. Use large 4-quart pot.

Venison And Potato Loaf

Categories: game

Yield: 5 servings

1 lb browned ground venison,

1 drained

4 c potatoes, peeled and sliced

1 tb onion, chopped

2 ts salt

1 pepper

3/4 c canned milk

1/2 c oats

1/4 c catsup

5 tb onion, chopped

Mix potatoes, 1 tablespoon onion, 1 teaspoon salt and dash of pepper (together and place in a 2 to 3 quart casserole. Then mix rest of ingredients together and spread this mixture over potatoes. Bake at 350F, covered, 30 to 45 minutes or until potatoes are tender.

Venison Hash

Categories: game

Yield: 5 servings

1 1/2 lb ground venison

3 lg onions, diced

1 lg green pepper, diced

1 cn 16 oz. tomatoes

2 ts salt

1/3 ts chili powder

1 sm red pepper, diced

1/2 c chopped chiles (optional)

Preheat over to 350F. In large skillet cook and stir venison, onions, and peppers until meat is brown and vegetables tender. Drain off the fat and stir in tomatoes, salt, pepper, chili powder, red pepper and chiles. Heat through and pour into covered casserole dish. Bake 1 hour stirring a couple times while cooking.

Venison Hamburger Rice Pie

Categories: meats, game

Yield: 5 servings

1 lb ground venison, browned

1 and drained 1/2 c bread crumbs

1/4 c green pepper, chopped

1/4 c onion, chopped

1 1/2 cn tomato sauce

2 1/2 c cooked rice

1/2 c grated cheese

1 salt and pepper to taste

Combine venison, bread crumbs, green pepper, onion and 1/2 can tomato sauce in large pie shell. Mix rice, cheese, salt and pepper and 1 can tomato sauce; place mixture on top of first mixture and spread other half can of tomato sauce over top. Bake in pie pan at 375F for about 35 minutes.

Savory Venison Chili

Categories: game, chili

Yield: 6 servings

1/4 lb slab bacon, cut into 1/4-dice

1 md onion, coarsely chopped

6 md carrots, peeled, halved-lengthwise; and cut into 1

2 ts chili powder

2 ts ground cumin

1 ts dried marjoram or oregano

1/4 ts red pepper flakes

2 lb venison shoulder, cut into-1/2 cubes

1 cn italian plum tomatoes, -crushed (28; oz)

1 1/2 c defatted chicken broth (or-beef bro; th)

1/2 c red wine

1/4 c tomato paste

1 cn dark-red kidney beans, -drained (16; oz)

1 c baby lima beans

3 c cooked rice or barley (opt)

I like to start off this chili with bacon. Once it browns, use 2 tablespoons of the bacon fat to wilt the vegetables - then one more tablespoon of the fat should be enough to brown the venison. Since the meat is lean, brown it quickly over high heat.

1. Brown the bacon in a skillet over medium heat for about 10 minutes or until golden brown. Remove bacon with a slotted spoon and set aside. Reserve 3 tablespoons of bacon fat; discard the rest.

2. Place 2 tablespoons of the bacon fat in a casserole;

add the onion and carrots, sprinkle with chili powder, cumin, marjoram and red pepper flakes, then cook for 5 minutes. Add the reserved bacon.

3. Pour the remaining tablespoon of bacon fat back into the skillet. Brown the venison over medium-high heat in small batches and remove to the casserole with a slotted spoon. (The meat should brown quickly, so raise the heat to high if necessary.)

4. Add the tomatoes, broth, wine and tomato paste. Bring to a simmer and cook, uncovered, for 40 minutes, stirring occasionally. Reduce the heat if the chili begins to boil.

5. Add the kidney beans and lima beans, then adjust the seasonings. Simmer 10 minutes longer or until meat is tender.

6. Serve the chili hot in 6 bowls (over rice or barley, if desired).

Venison Chili Ala Fred

Categories: game, chili

Yield: 4 servings

1 lb venson [ground]

1/2 c onions [chopped]

1/2 ts salt

1/4 ts pepper

4 c tomatoes [canned & chopped]

3/4 c catsup

1 cn (15« oz) kidney beans

1) Combine the venison, onions, salt and pepper, and brown in a skillet, stirring `til crumbley. . . 2) Add the remaining ingredients, and simmer for 45 min or `til it is of the desired consistancy. . .

Don's Venison Chili

Categories: meats, game, chili

Yield: 6 servings

4 lb boneless, cubed venison

2 jalapenos seeded & chopped

3 tb bacon grease

3 tb soy sauce

5 tb fresh ground cumin

1/2 c chopped green bell pepper

5 garlic cloves minced

2 onions chopped

1 1/2 cans of beer [*not lite]

8 oz can tomato sauce

1/2 ts cayenne pepper

2 c stewed tomatos

6 jalapenos fresh & whole

2 tb masa harina

1/2 ts salt

1 oz jack daniels whiskey

Brown meat in bacon grease. Saute the onions, the chopped jalapenos, & the Bell peppers in the bacon grease until the onions start to become transparent. Meanwhile bring the beer & whiskey to a boil and add the meat, seasonings, except for 1 Tblpsn of cumin, & the onions/peppers to the pot.

Allow to boil for 5-7 minutes. Reduce the heat to medium then add the tomatos & tomato sauce. Stir occassionally while continuing to cook for 30 minutes. reduce heat to simmer and cook for 1 hour.

Oven-Barbecued Venison Ribs

Categories: main dish, meats, game

Yield: 8 servings

2 lb venison ribs

1 vegetable oil

1 salt & pepper

2 tb vinegar

2 tb brown sugar

1 ts prepared mustard

16 oz tomato sauce

In a 2-qt. baking dish or roaster arrange ribs. Brush lightly with cooking oil & sprinkle with salt & pepper. Bake at 325-350 degrees until fairly well done, turning once. Pour off any juices. Combine vinegar, brown sugar & mustard with tomato sauce & pour over ribs. Bake until done, basting occasionally with sauce.

Venison Suey

Categories: main dish, meats, game, beef

Yield: 4 servings

1 lb steak, cut in thin strips

2 tb oil

4 oz drained mushrooms

1 1/2 c sliced celery

1 c sliced green pepper

1/2 c sliced onion *

2 tb soy sauce

2 tb cornstarch

1/2 c water

In skillet, brown venison steak in oil. Add vegetables, soup & soy sauce. Cover, cook over low heat 20 min. or until meat is tender. Stir now & then. Blend cornstarch & water then stir into meat & vegetables. Cook, stirring until thickened. Serve with hot rice. * onions can be substituted with 1 can beef or onion soup for every 1/2 cup onions

Venison Rib Barbecue

Categories: main dish, meats, game, sauces

Yield: 4 servings

----MARINADE----

1 c sugar

1/4 c vinegar

1/4 c salt

1 slice of bacon

1 slice of onion

1/4 ts chili powder

-BARBECUE SAUCE-

1 ea chopped onion

6 oz tomato juice

1/2 ts oregano

1/2 ts basil

1/2 ts marjoram

1 ea stalk of celery

1 ea chopped carrot

Clean as much fat off ribs as you can. Marinate overnight. Dry pieces & roll in flour, fry until light brown. Remove from skillet & arrange in a large fry pan or skillet. Cover with barbecue sauce & bake until tender at 350 degrees.

Venison Pepper Steak

Yield: 8 servings

2 lb venison steak, cut in strips

----MIXTURE

1/2 c flour

3/4 ts salt

1/4 ts pepper

1/2 c shortening

1 cn stewed tomatoes, save juice

3/4 c chopped onion

2 c water

1/2 ts garlic powder

2 ea beef bouillon cubes

3 ea green peppers, cut in strips

2 ts worcestershire sauce

Melt shortening in large skillet. Roll venison in flour mixture, using all the mixture. Brown meat in hot shortening, add the liquid from tomatoes, water, onion, garlic powder & bouillon cubes. Cover & simmer 1 1/2-2 hrs.

Uncover, stir in worcestershire sauce, add pepper strips, cover & cook 10 minutes more. Add the tomatoes, cook until tomatoes are hot (about 5 minutes). Serve over hot cooked rice. This makes a delicious hunting camp supper, served with tossed salad, hot garlic bread, & fruit for dessert.

Onion Buttered Deer Steak

Categories: meats, game, beef

Yield: 1 servings

--BUTTER SAUCE--

1/2 c butter

1/4 c minced onion

2 ts worcestershire or soy sauce

1/2 ts dry mustard

1/2 ts freshly ground pepper

In small saucepan, combine ingredients. Heat together until butter melts. Broil 3 to 4 inches from heat for 10 to 12 minutes each side for rare, 14 to 16 minutes for medium, brushing with butter mixture.

Venison Roast Burgundy

Yield: 12 servings

6 lb roast

1 ea celery stalk with leaves

2 ea carrots, quartered

1/2 c dry red wine

2 ea med. onions, quartered

1 salt & pepper

1 ea crumbled bay leaf

1/2 ts rosemary

1/2 ts marjoram

Place roast in center of piece of heavy aluminum foil large enough to completely wrap it. Put in shallow pan; fold foil up around meat pan fashion.

Brown under broiler. Add vegetables; brush them with melted butter or fat & brown also. Season meat with salt, pepper & herbs. Add wine. Bring foil up around meat & seal the edges with a double fold. Place in 300 degree oven for about 3 1/2 hrs. (If longer time is available, roast in 250 degree oven for about 4 1/2 hrs.). Remove meat to a hot platter. Simmer juices in saucepan until slightly thickened, correct seasonings & serve.

Venison Chops And Rice

Categories: main dish, rice, game

Yield: 6 servings

6 ea chops

6 tb uncooked rice

6 ea slices onion

6 ea slices tomato

1 cn chicken broth

Brown chops on both sides. Grease casserole dish well. Put 1 tb rice for each chop in bottom of dish.

Place chops on rice. Put slice of onion, tomato & pepper on each chop. Cover with chicken broth. Bake 1 hr. at 350 degrees.

Venison Chops In Tomato Soup

Categories: main dish, meats, game

Yield: 4 servings

8 ea chops

1 salt & pepper

1 garlic powder

1 cn tomato soup

1/2 ea green pepper, chopped

1/2 ea med. onion

1 1/3 c minute rice

Put salt, pepper & garlic powder on chops. Brown in oil in electric skillet. Pour tomato soup in skillet.

Add green peppers & onions. Simmer 1 or 1 1/2 hrs.

Turn skillet off & add minute rice. Let stand until sauce is absorbed.

Venison Jerky

Categories: game

Yield: 1 servings

2 lb venison

1 c soy sauce

1 ts lemon juice

1/2 ts black pepper

1/4 ts garlic

Cut the venison in strips approximately 1/4 x 1 x 8-inches. Mix all ingredients and marinate venison approximately 10 hours turning once every hour. Smoke venison on grill until completely dry or you may use oven on low heat with venison spread out on broiler pan.

Deer Jerky

Categories: game

Yield: 1 servings

4 lb venison

4 tb onion powder

1 1/2 ts black pepper

1 1/2 ts garlic powder

2 pinches salt

1/2 ts italian seasoning

1 c worcestershire sauce

1 c soy sauce

1 ts texas pete

Serves many people.

Cut venison into 1/3-inch strips or less, cutting with the grain. Combine rest of ingredients. Place meat in pan or dish and pour marinade over meat. Let stand 24 hours in refrigerator. Remove from refrigerator and place foil in bottom of oven to catch drippings. Insert toothpicks through one end of strip of meat and hang from over rack. Rack should be at highest setting. Bake at 150F for 4 hours or until dried to taste.

Smoked Oriental Venison Jerky

Categories: game

Yield: 1 servings

4 lb venison roast

1/4 c salt

1/4 c brown sugar

2 c water

1 c apple cider/or cider vinegar

1/2 c soy sauce

2 oz bourbon or brandy

1/2 ts onion powder

1/2 ts garlic powder

1 ts grated ginger

1 ts grated orange peel

6 white cloves (optional)

Serves many people.

Trim fat from venison and cut into 1/4- to 1/2-inch thick slices. Place meat into the marinade made by combining the above ingredients in a glass or ceramic bowl. Marinate at least 8 hours in a cool place. Remove to a rack and allow to air dry until they become glazed. Do not rinse. Smoke for

12 to 16 hours depending on degree of desired dryness. Use approximately 3 panfuls of hickory or cherry wood chips to add flavor.

Hearty Venison Soup

Categories: soups, game

Yield: 6 servings

4 tb corn oil

1 lb venison, cubed

1 lb sweet italian sausage

28 oz can tomatoes

3 c water

1 c chopped onions

1 tb worcestershire sauce

2 potatoes, peeled, cubed

1 c celery, sliced

In large kettle, heat oil, add venison, and brown all sides. Remove meat with a slotted spoon and set aside. Add sausage, sliced, to kettle and brown on all sides. Drain off drippings. Add tomatoes (broken up with a spoon), water, onion, Worcestershire sauce, and browned venison. Heat to boiling. Reduce heat to simmer, cover and cook until almost tender - about 1 1/2 hours. Add cubed potatoes and sliced celery and simmer until vegetables and meat are tender, about 1 hour more.

Venison Cheese Ball Soup

Categories: soups, game

Yield: 6 servings

1 lb ground venison

1 tb margarine

1 md onion, chopped

1 clove garlic, minced

1 (28 ounce) can whole-tomatoes, mashed

18 oz of tomato juice

1 (15 ounce) can tomato sauce

1 (15 ounce) can pinto beans

1 tb worcestershire sauce

1 ts basil

1 ds pepper

2 eggs

1/2 c grated parmesan cheese

1/2 ts thyme leaves

1/2 c finely rolled saltine-cracker crumbs

4 c shredded cabbage

Brown meat in margarine and set aside to cool. Place onion, garlic, tomatoes, tomato juice, tomato sauce, beans, Worcestershire, basil and pepper in large covered kettle. Bring to a boil, cover and simmer for 30 minutes. Combine eggs, Parmesan, thyme, crackers and browned venison. Mix well. Shape into 1-inch balls. When soup has simmered for 30 minutes, stir in cabbage and drop in venison cheese balls. Cover and simmer for another 30 minutes

Venison Goulash Soup

Categories: soups, game

Yield: 12 servings

5 1/2 lb lean venison, cut into

1-1/4-inch cubes

5 oz lard

5 1/2 lb onions, sliced

5 oz sweet paprika

1 tb hot paprika

1 1/4 qt red wine

3 1/8 qt water

2 lg potatoes, peeled and quartered

3 carrots, peeled and quartered

2 apples, peeled, cored and quartered

1 peppercorns

1 juniper berries

3 bay leaves

1 a few chili seeds

3 stalks celery, thinly sliced

2 bn parsley, chopped

1 sour cream to taste

Best made in large quantities. Recipe therefor serves 12.

In a large pot, melt some of the lard and brown the meat in batches. Add more lard as required. Remove the meat and reserve. Fry onions until browned. Remove onions from pot and reserve. Add remaining lard. Add paprika and stir well. Slowly add red wine and water, continuing to stir to make sure there are no lumps of paprika. Add meat and onions to pot again. Add potatoes, carrots, apples and spices. Quantities are approximate, use more, or less, as you wish. Cook gently, covered, for 3 hours. Check occasionally, and add more water as required. Remove coarse spices, and add celery and parsley. Serve with a bowl of sour cream, so each person can help themselves.

Uncle Buck's Venison Kabobs

Yield: 1 servings

1 venison; kabobs

1/4 c cranberry juice

1/4 c olive oil

1/4 ts fresh garlic

1/4 ts onion salt

1/4 ts celery salt

1/4 ts black pepper

1/4 ts sweet basil

1/8 ts ginger

1 mushroom

1 onions

1 green peppers

1 cherry tomatoes

Recipe by: Uncle Buck's Venison, Littleton, NH Mix juice, oil and spices. Marinate the venison kabobs overnight or at least 4 hours in the refrigerat

Thread the kabob on skewers. Alternate skewered meat with mushrooms, onion and green peppers. Grill over hot fire for several minutes. Do not overcoo

While cooking, baste meat and vegetables several times with leftover marina Serve on a warmed platter.

Dutch Oven Venison

Categories: meats, game

Yield: 4 servings

4 lb shoulder roast of venison

1 flour seasoned with salt and

1 pepper

3 tb cooking oil

1 onion, sliced

1 green pepper, sliced

1 garlic clove, minced

1 cn tomatoes (16-oz)

1 tb sugar

1/2 c dry red wine

1/2 ts thyme

1 parsley sprig

4 cloves, whole

20 peppercorns

2 bay leaves, crushed

12 juniper berries, crushed

Marinate meat overnight in whole milk. Discard marinade. Pat dry. Roll roast in seasoned flour and brown in hot cooking oil in Dutch oven. When brown on all sides, remove the roast from the pot. In the same pan, saute the onion, green pepper, and garlic over moderate heat for 5 minutes, stirring often. Add tomatoes, sugar, wine, and thyme to the Dutch oven and heat. Place the parsley, cloves, peppercorns, and bay leaves on a piece of double-thickness cheese cloth, and tie with a string into a bag. Add the bag to pot. When the mixture is boiling, add the browned roast and baste with sauce. Cover and cook at 350 degrees F. for about 2 1/2 hours, until tender. Baste several times with pan juices during the roasting, slice thinly, and serve with pan juices.

Stuffed Venison Pinwhells

Yield: 8 servings

2 whole venison backstraps, 1 rolled out 1/4 in. thick

1 qt whole milk

2 ts wild game seasoning

1 lb velveeta cheese

1 cn rotel tomatoes with diced

1 chiles

2 lb thinly sliced lean bacon

1/2 c thinly sliced green onions

8 cloves garlic, finely mince

First, prepare the backstrap fillet. It's an extremely tender tubelike piece of meat about 12 inches long and 2 to 3 inches in diameter. And because of its shape, it can be cut around the perimeter, 1/4 inch thick, and rolled out flat. To do this, you need a very sharp knife. Start by laying out the fillet perpendicular to your body and making a shallow slice about 1/4 inch deep in the meat. Then, as if slicing through and unrolling paper towels from a roll, begin working around the outside perimeter of the fillet until the backstrap comes out looking like a round steak. It takes a little practice to do . . . but you can do it! When the meat is ready, place both pieces into a glass or plastic container and cover them with whole milk. You want to marinate the venison for at least 6 hours, but preferably overnight. The milk tenderizes the deer and helps to remove any unwanted gamey flavor. After the marination process, remove the meat from the milk (you can discard the milk), and pat the venison dry with several paper towels. Then liberally sprinkle both sides with wild game seasoning and rub it briskly into the meat. At this point, preheat your oven to 400 degrees.

Then, in your food processor, mix together the Velveeta cheese and the Rotel tomatoes until smooth and creamy. When you're ready to make the pinwheels, spread a thin layer of the cheese mixture evenly over one side of the deer. Then place a layer of bacon strips - side by side - on top of the cheese. Finish up the preparation by lightly sprinkling on a little sliced green onions and a little minced garlic. Now tightly roll up the flattened fillets and set them aside momentarily. Then on the same work surface, lay out another 8 to 10 strips of bacon side by side and put one of the rolled backstraps on top of them. Now wrap the bacon strips around the venison and pin them in place with toothpicks. When you are finished, the backstrap should be completely encased in bacon strips. Repeat with the other backstrap. All that's left is to take a sharp knife, slice the rolled venison into 2 inch thick pinwheels, position them on a shallow cookie sheet, and bake them - uncovered - in the oven for about 40 to 45 minutes.

You'll notice that a light sauce will form in the bottom of the cookie sheet; you can use this to baste the pinwheels as they cook. The one thing you don't want to do is overcook the venison - it will come out dry and chewy instead of juicy and tender if you do! Note: If you don't have wild game seasoning on hand, you can lightly sprinkle the venison with salt, black pepper, onion powder, garlic powder, and sweet basil as a substitute.

Uncle Buck's Venison Chili

Yield: 8 servings

2 tb olive oil

1 md bell pepper; chopped

2 md onions; chopped fine

2 cl garlic; crushed

1 lb venison; ground

1 lb venison; cut in chunks

8 oz tomatoes; canned

4 tb tomato paste

1 bay leaf

1 ts ground cumin

1 ts oregano

1/4 ts cayenne pepper

1 tb chili powder; mild

1 salt and pepper; to taste

1 c beef stock

2 tb dark brown sugar; to taste

2 cn chili pepperssmall

14 oz red kidney beans, canned

Heat olive oil in large saucepan. Add onions, garlic and bell peppers. Fry until soft. Brown allmeat and add to above.

Stir in tomatoes, tomato paste, seasonings and beef stock with a wooden spoon.

Bring to a boil. Reduce Heat to low and cover. Add chili peppers. Simmer for two hours, stirring occasionally. Add kidney beans and simmer for another 30 minutes. Remove bay leaf and serve.

Venison With Green Peppercorns

Categories: game

Yield: 4 servings

4 venison fillets (6 oz ea)

1 tb green peppercorns

3 oz bourbon whiskey

1 salt

1 freshly ground pepper

1 chopped shallot

1/4 c red wine

1/4 c heavy cream

2 tb butter

1 tb chopped fresh chives, thyme-or pars; ley

Soak green peppercorns in bourbon for 30 minutes or longer.

Heat butter in a saute pan. Salt and pepper the venison on both sides and saute quickly, about 2 minutes per side (depending on thickness) for medium rare. Remove from pan and keep warm.

Add shallots to pan juices; cook 1 minute. Add green peppercorns and bourbon; boil 1 minute. Add wine and cook down to a fine glaze. Add heavy cream and continue cooking until sauce coats the back of a spoon. Add herbs and any meat juices. Serve sauce over venison.

Venison Burgers

Categories: game

Yield: 8 burgers

1 lb ground venison

3 oz pork fat back, ground

1 salt

1 freshly ground pepper

Because venison has so little fat, you'll need to add some for a juicy burger. But don't use deer fat - it tastes bad.)

Mix venison, pork, salt and pepper, handling as little as possible. Heat grill. Brush burgers with vegetable oil and grill about 4 minutes; turn and cook to desired doneness. Serve on rolls with your choice of condiments.

Fiery Barbecued Venison

Categories: game, barbeque

Yield: 4 servings

4 venison steaks or medallions - (about; 4 oz. per portion)

2 ts paprika

1 ts chili powder

1 ts ground cumin

1 ts ground coriander (cilantro)

1 ts sugar

1 ts salt

1/2 ts dry mustard powder

1/2 ts dried thyme leaves

1/2 ts good curry powder

1/2 ts cayenne

-CORIANDER AVACADO CREAM--

1/2 avacado (~ 4 tablespoon)

3 tb sour cream

2 tb fresh chopped coriander

1/2 ts grated lime peel

4 dr tabasco sauce

1 salt

1 pepper

1 olive oil for basting

This Southwestern-style dish from the Cervena venison people packs an intense flavor punch.

To make the avacado cream, place all ingredients in a processor or blender and blend until smooth.

Combine all the meat spices in a large bowl. Place the venison in the bowl and mix to coat well. Brush off excess coating and let stand 1 hour.

Heat the barbecue grill; oil the grill.

Brown venison well over high heat, turning often and basting lightly with olive oil. When done to your taste, remove from grill, cover with foil and let stand about 5 minutesserve with coriander cream.

Oriental Venison Cutlets

Categories: game, asian

Yield: 8 servings

16 venison cutlets (3 oz ea)

2 tb olive oil

1 tb fresh chopped basil

1 tb fresh chopped chervil

1 tb fresh chopped cilantro

1 tb fresh chopped mint

1 tb fresh chopped flat parsley

2 tb sesame oil

1 tb chopped carlic

2 tb chopped shallots

2 tb unpeeled grated ginger

2 tb soy sauce

1 1/2 c chicken broth

1 tb butter

In a large skillet, heat olive oil over medium high heat. Sear cutlets quickly to desired doneness; remove from pan and keep warm. Mix herbs together; coat each cutlet with sesame oil and herbs.

Add garlic, shallots, ginger, soy sauce and chicken stock to pan juices. Simmer about 8 minutes. Swirl in butter; return to simmer. Arrange venison slices on plates and spoon sauce over each. Serve immediately.

Big Bob's Shoulder Of Venison

Categories: game

Yield: 6 servings

1 5 lb. shoulder of venison

1 ts pepper

1 ts allspice

1/4 c butter [softened]

1 lg onion [chopped]

1 cn (12 oz) beer

1 c sour cream

1 cn cream of mushroom soup

1) Season venison with the spices, rubbing in lightly, then spread the butter on the meat, covering completely. Place the roast in a 8" x 13" roasting pan and cover with the onions. . . 2) Combine the beer, sour cream, and soup in a bowl and wisk `til blended, then pour over the roast. . . 3) Bake in a 300ø oven for 1« hours `til meat is fork tender (adding small amounts of water if necessary) * Thicken the pan drippings for gravy if desired. . . Serve with noodles, rice or potatoes.

Marinated Venison

Categories: game

Yield: 12 servings

2 lg carrots [sliced]

2 lg onions [sliced]

2 celery stalks [finely 1 chopper]

1/2 c olive oil

2 garlic cloves

2 ts salt

1 ts pepper [fresh ground]

1/2 c sugar

1/2 ts cloves

1/2 ts allspice

1/2 ts basil

2 bay leaves

1/2 tb parsley [chopped]

4 c vinegar

4 c water

2 c beer

4 lb venison shoulder [cubed]

1) Saut, the carrots, onions, and celery in 1 tb ov olive oil in a skillet over low heat for 15 min. , stirring frequently. Add the remaining olive oil, garlic, salt, pepper, sugar, cloves, allspice, basil, bay leaves, parsley vinegar, water, and beer, mixing well, and pour into a nonreactive bowl. . . Add the venison and marinate in the refrigerator for 24 to 48 hours stirring occasionally. . . 2) Place the venison in w/marinade in a stock pot and bring to a boil

over med to low heat then reduce heat to low and simmer for 2 hours. . . 3) Discard the bay leaves, thicken the pan juices for gravy and serve

Venison Steaks With Chestnuts & Figs

Categories: game

Yield: 4 servings

1 stephen ceideburg

1/2 tb butter

1 black pepper

50 g chopped green onions

200 ml port wine

300 ml stock

24 peeled chestnuts

1 tb butter

8 venison medallions

4 figs

By rights, this dish requires lengthy preparation of a stock made with the bones and trimmings of venison. However, this is impossible for most of us who buy venison as a boneless fillet.

A good beef stock is a satisfactory substitute and if you use a canned beef bouillon (Campbells makes one) and prepare the chestnuts in advance, the meal can be prepared very rapidly.

Melt half a tablespoon of butter in a heavy saucepan, add a good grinding of black pepper and gently cook 50 g chopped green (spring) onions. Add 200 mL port and reduce. Add 300 mL stock and 24 peeled chestnuts and simmer for about 20 minutes or until the sauce becomes syrupy. Set aside and keep warm.

Heat a heat a heavy-based frying pan, add a tablespoon of butter. When it is very hot, cook 8 medallions of venison, each about 1 cm thick.

Sear them for a maximum of 1 minute on each side, to ensure they are still rare.

Meanwhile, butter a baking tray and slice onto it 4 figs. Place under a grill to heat through.

Divide the sauce and chestnuts between four heated plates and add to each plate 2 medallions of venison and a fan of fig slices. Serve immediately.

Marinated Loin Of Venison Roasted In Mustard

Categories: game

Yield: 8 servings

1 stephen ceideburg

1 pt basic liquid game marinade-(see recipe)

4 to 5-pound boneless loin of venison; , well trimmed

3 lg garlic cloves

1/3 c chopped green onions

1/3 c dry white wine

1 ts chopped fresh sage

1 ts fresh thyme (or 1/2 teaspoon- dried)

1 c dijon mustard

1/4 c olive oil

1 ts kosher or sea salt

Pour marinade over venison in a glass or stainless-steel pan. Cover and refrigerate 1 to 2 hours, turning occasionally.

Remove venison from marinade and pat dry. Discard marinade. Quickly sear the meat in a hot saute pan of on a grill for 3 to 4 minutes. If necessary, cut loin in half and sear in 2 batches.

Place remaining ingredients in a food processor or blender, and quickly process until smooth. Mixture should be very thick. Cover and refrigerate.

Place venison in a roasting pan and coat well with the mustard mixture. Roast in a preheated 375 degree F. oven for 12 to 15 minutes, or until meat is medium rare (130 degrees F. internal temperature).

Let meat rest at least 5 minutes before carving.

Venison Stew

Categories: soups, game

Yield: 6 servings

1 lb venison [cubed]

2 tb oil

6 c water

1 c onions [chopped]

1 c peas

1 c green beans

4 lg potatoes [peeled & chopped]

1 1/2 c carrots [sliced]

1 c corn

1 ts salt

1/4 ts pepper

2 bay leaves

3 tb cornstarch

1 c cold water

1) Brown the venison in the oil in a stock pot then drain.

2) Add the 6 cups of water, the veggies, salt and pepper, and bay leaves, cooking over med. heat for 45 min. to an hour or `til the meat and veggies are tender.

3) Combine the cornstarch and the remaining water in a small bowl, and stir into the stew `til thickened, stirring constantly.

4) Remove and discard the bay leaves. . . Serve. . .

Venison Nacho Dip

Categories: game

Yield: 6 servings

1 stephen ceideburg

1 lb ground venison

1/2 onion, minced

1 salt and pepper to taste

16 oz refried beans

2 oz chopped green chiles

1 1/2 c grated cheddar cheese

6 oz mild taco sauce

3 green onions, chopped

10 ripe olives sliced

1 c sour cream

1 c guacamole

1 tortilla chips

Cook meat and onion in a nonstick pan until meat browns and onion is soft. Season with salt and pepper.

Spread the refried beans in a flat 10-inch casserole dish. Layer the meat over the beans. Sprinkle chopped chiles over the meat. Cover with grated cheese and taco sauce.

Bake at 400 degrees F. for 25 minutes. Remove from oven and sprinkle with green onions and olives.

Venison Goulash

Categories: game, camping, neysa

Yield: 6 servings

2 tb oil

1 1/2 lb venison, from neck, flank,

1 shanks, cut into cubes 1 to 1 1 1/2 inches

3 md onions, very thinly sliced

2 tb paprika

1 ts salt

1 md green bell pepper, thinly

1 sliced, seeds & pith removed

1/2 c water

In a Dutch Oven, heat oil and brown venison, stirring often. Add the onions, sprinkle with paprika and salt while stirring, saute over med heat until onions are soft. Put in the green pepper and water, cover the Dutch Oven but do not put coals on top. Cook 1 to 1 1/2 hours, until the venison is fork tender. Traditionally Goulash is served with broad noodles.

Venison Sausage Balls

Categories: appetizers, game, southern

Yield: 5 servings

1 1/2 lb venison; ground

1/2 c breadcrumbs, dry

1 egg; beaten

1 ts salt

1/2 c potatoes; mashed

1/2 ts sugar, brown

1/4 ts pepper

1/4 ts allspice, ground

1/4 ts nutmeg, ground

1/8 ts cloves, ground

1/8 ts ginger, ground

1/4 c butter (or marg.); melted

1 orange slices; opt.

1 lemon slices; opt.

1 parsley sprigs; opt.

Combine first 11 ingredients, mixing well. Shape into 1" balls. Brown well in butter, stirring occasionally. Cover and cook over low heat 15 minutes. Arrange on serving platter; garnish with fruit and parsley, if desired.

Venison Pot Roast

Yield: 5 servings

7 lb boned leg-of-venison roast

1 3 to 6 bacon slices

2 c burgandy

1/2 c cider vinegar

2 celery tops

1 md onion, sliced

4 lemon slices

1 lg carrot, pared and sliced

1 tb salt

10 whole black peppers

2 bay leaves

1 clove garlic, crushed

1/4 c unsifted all-purpose flour

2 tb salad oil

Wipe roast with damp paper towels. Arrange bacon slices over inside surface of meat; roll up, and tie securely.

Combine Burgandy, vinegar, celery tops, onion, lemon slices, carrot, salt, black peppers, bay leaves, and garlic with one cup water.

Pour over roast in a large bowl. Refrigerate, covered, 24 hours, turning occasionally.

Remove roast from marinade; reserve 2 cups marinade. Coat roast well with flour. Slowly heat oil in Dutch oven.

Add roast; cook, over medium heat, until browned all over-about 20 minutes.

Add 1 cup reserved marinade; bring to boiling. Reduce

heat, and simmer, covered, 4 hours, or until roast is fork-tender. Baste meat occasionally with pan liquid, adding rest of marinade as needed.

Deer Sausage

Categories: game

Yield: 1 servings

2 lb bacon, smoked, unsliced

5 lb venison, lean

1 tb sage, rubbed

1 tb smoked salt

Grind meats, blending together thoroughly with salt and sage. Smoke in links or cook in patties in a pan.

Roast Loin Of Venison With Savory Wine Sauce

Categories: game, ethnic

Yield: 6 servings

1 c olive oil

1/2 c carrot; finely chopped

1/2 c celery; finely chopped

1/2 c onion; finely chopped

4 cl garlic; minced

2 sprigs fresh thyme

2 bay leaves

3 lb loin of venison, with bone

2 tb clarified butter

1 salt to taste

1 fresh ground black pepper

1 savory wine sauce:

3 c beef stock

2 tb butter

1 reserved venison bones

1/4 c minced shallots

1 cl garlic; minced

1 sprig thyme

2 tomatoes; coarsely chopped

3 tb sherry wine vinegar

1/4 c port

2 tb red currant jelly

1 salt to taste

1 fresh ground black pepper

Make a marinade of the first 7 ingredients. Bone the loin; trim and discard fat and sinew. With a cleaver chop the bone into 1" pieces and reserve for the sauce. Slice loin against the grain into 6 pieces. Arrange in a single layer in a casserole dish. Pour over the marinade, cover and refrigerate 24 hours. Meanwhile prepare the sauce. Bring stock to a boil, reduce heat and cook uncovered until volume reduced by 1/2. Set aside. Melt butter in a large, heavy saucepan over high heat. Add bones; brown quickly, stirring often. Add shallots, garlic and thyme, cooking until soft and lightly colored. Add tomato; cook several more minutes. Add wines and vinegar, bring to a boil and reduce by half. Add stock and currant jelly. Reduce heat to low, cover, and simmer 1 hour, skimming as necessary. Remove from heat, strain and return to clean pan. Salt and pepper. Refrigerate until needed and reheat before serving. To cook the venison, remove from marinade, pat dry, and season with salt and pepper. Sautee in clarified butter, searing all sides quickly. Transfer pan to preheated 400 deg oven for 5-7 minutes until medium rare. Slice each piece against the grain into 3-4 pieces and serve with the reheated sauce.

Venison Mincemeat Pie

Yield: 8 servings

2 c apple cider or apple juice

1 c dark seedless raisins

1/2 c dried sour or sweet cherries or cur; rants

1 1/2 c chopped, peeled apples

1/4 lb ground venison or lean-ground beef

1 ts ground cinnamon

1 ts ground cloves

1 ts ground ginger

1/2 ts salt

1/2 ts ground nutmeg

1/4 ts ground allspice

1 pastry (recipe follows)

1. At least 4 hours before making pie, prepare the mincemeat: In heavy

2-quart saucepan, combine cider, raisins, and cherries. Cover and heat to boiling over high heat. Reduce heat to low and simmer 30 minutes, stirring occasionally.

2. Add apples, venison, cinnamon, cloves, ginger, salt, nutmeg, and allspice. Simmer 2 hours longer. Check occasion- ally and add water if necessary to keep mincemeat from sticking to saucepan. Cool mincemeat to room temperature. (Mincemeat can be made up to 3 months ahead and frozen. If frozen, thaw mincemeat before making pie or baking time will be lengthened.)

3. Meanwhile, prepare pastry and refrigerate until ready to use-at least 30 minutes.

4. Heat oven to 350'F. Divide pastry into 3 equal pieces.

Press 2 pieces together and shape into a ball. Between 2 sheets of waxed paper, roll out ball of pastry into an 11 - inch round. Remove top sheet of paper and invert pastry into 9- inch pie plate, letting excess extend over edge. Remove bottom sheet of paper.

5. Between sheets of waxed paper, roll out remaining pastry to a 9 1/2- by 6-inch rectangle. Remove top sheet of paper from pastry. Cut rectangle into four 9 1/2- by 1 1/2-inch strips.

6. Carefully spoon mincemeat into crust-lined pie plate. Remove pastry strips from waxed paper, one at a time, and place across mincemeat to create spokes. All four strips will overlap in the center. Lift edge of bottom crust over ends of strips. Pinch together and flute edge. Place pie on rimmed baking sheet.

7. Bake pie 50 to 55 minutes or until crust is lightly browned and filling bubbles. Cool 10 minutes on wire rack before cutting.

Pastry: In medium-size bowl, combine 1 1/2 C unsifted all-purpose flour and 1/2 t salt. With pastry blender or 2 knives, cut in 1/3 C vegetable shortening, chilled, until mixture resembles coarse crumbs. Add 5 to 6 T cold water to flour mixture and mix lightly with fork until moistened; gather into a ball. Wrap pastry and refrigerate 30 minutes.

Lillie Bell's Venison Roast

Yield: 6 servings

5 lb to 7 pound venison roast

1/4 c salt (yep, 1/4 cup)

1 ts seasoned salt

1 ts garlic powder

1 ts pepper

1 ts soy sauce

1 ea onionsliced

2 tb all-purpose flour

1/4 c butter or margarine

1 qt to 2 qt water; divided

1 all-purpose flour

Combine roast, water to cover, and 1/4 cup salt in a large Dutch oven. Cover and let soak 2 hours. Drain, rinse, and pat dry.

Combine seasoned salt, garlic powder, and peppersprinkle on both sides of roast. Sprinkle with soy sauce. Place onion slices on top of roast, and sprinkle with 2 tablespoons flour. Place pats of butter on onion. Wrap roast twice in heavy-duty aluminum-foil. Place in roasting pan; add 1 quart water. Cover and bake at 350 degrees F for 4 to 5 hours. Add water, if necessary, to roasting pan, but do not open foil.

Remove roast from pan. Carefully open foil, and measure liquid. Combine 1-1/2 tablespoons flour and 2 tablespoons water for each cup of liquidstir well. Stir in lour mixture. Cook over medium heat, stirring constantly, until thickened and bubbly. Serve gravy with roast.

Note: remove as much fat as possible before cooking to eliminate any gamey flavor.

Smoked Venison Roast

Categories: game

Yield: 6 servings

1 water pan seasonings:

1 c white wine - dry

1 onion - medium, whole

1 bell pepper - halved and peeled

1 garlic clove - large, whole

2 tb parsley - dried

1 ts dried mint - crushed

6 drops peychaud's bitters or, 3 drops angostura bitter 2 tb lea & perrins-worcestershire, sauce 1 tb liquid smoke

Instructions:

DIRECTIONS

Prepare the smoker as you would for any other roast. Put the ingredients listed above in the water pan.

To cook venison, it is important to remove the fat and membrane from the meat. I stick a knife in the meat, then push some peeled cloves of garlic into the slit. You can push whole fresh cayenne peppers and green onions in the slit also.

After stuffing the slits you have made, sprinkle salt over the surface and pat in. Do the same with red cayenne pepper.

Mushroom- Crusted Venison Loin

Categories: game

Yield: 8 servings

3 1/4 oz shiitake mushrooms

8 oz fresh cremini mushrooms

1/4 c olive oil

1 ts sea salt

1/2 ts pepper

1 lb skinned chicken breasts

1/4 c parsley leaves

1/4 c fresh chervil leaves

20 oz boneless venison loin

Garnishes grilled purple onion strips, asparagus spears, sweet red pepper strips. Wash mushroom thoroughly; remove and discard shiitake stems. Place oil in a large skillet; add mushrooms, salt & pepper. Cover & cook until mushrooms are tender. Drain & set aside the mushrooms. Position knife blade in food processor bowl; add chicken & process until finely chopped, stopping occasionally to scrape down sides. Add mushrooms, parsley & chervil; process until mix is thoroughly blended, stopping occasionally to scrape down sides. Cut 2 sheet of heavy-duty plastic wrap long enough to fit around deer meat. Place chicken mix on 1 sheet & top with remaining sheet roll mix to about 1/4 in thickness covering entire sheet remove top layer of plastic. Place deer in center of chicken mix, cover entire deer with chicken mix ; remove plastic wrap & place deer seam side down on a greased baking sheet. Bake at 350 until meat thermometer get to 150 checking temp after first 10 mins. Garnish if desired, Yield 8 servings.

Grilled Venison Steaks

Yield: 10 servings

12 lb to 14 pound venison hind--quarter

16 oz bottle commercial italian-dressing

2 3/4 oz package dry onion soup mix

3/4 c butter or margarine; melted

2 ts pepper

Separate each muscle of the hindquarter, and cut away from bone. Slice each muscle across the grain into 1-inch thick slices (reserve remaining meat for use in another recipe). Remove and discard the white membrane surrounding each steak.

Combine salad dressing and soup mix in a large, shallow dish, stirring well; add steaks. Cover and marinate steaks in refrig- erator for one hour, turning once.

Combine butter and pepper, stirring wellset aside. Remove steaks from marinade. Grill about 5 inches from hot coals 8 to 10 minutes on each side or until done, basting occasionally with butter mixture.

Yield: 10 to 12 servings.

Country-Style Venison Steaks

Yield: 10 servings

12 lb to 14 lb venison hindquarter

1 1/2 c all purpose flour

1 1/2 ts salt

3/4 ts pepper

3/4 c vegetable oil

3/4 ts rubbed sage; divided

3/4 ts dried whole thyme; divided

3 md onionssliced and divided

4 1/2 c ; water

Separate each muscle of the hindquarter, and cut away from the bone. Slice each muscle across the grain into 1-inch thick slices (reserve remaining meat for use in another recipe). Remove and discard the white membrane surrounding each steakset steaks aside.

Combine flour, salt, and pepperstir well. Dredge venison in flour mixture and reserve remaining flour mixture. Brown meat on both sides in hot oil in a large Dutch oven. Remove meat from Dutch oven, and discard drippings.

Layer one-third of steaks in Dutch ovensprinkle with 1/4 teaspoon sage and 1/4 teaspoon thyme. Top with one-third of onion slices. Repeat layers twice; using remaining steaksspices, and onion.

Gradually add water to reserved flour mixture, stirring until smooth; pour over steaks. Cover and simmer 1 to 1-1/2 hours or until tender.

Yield: 10 to 12 servings.

Venison Kabobs

Yield: 6 servings

2 lg green peppers; quartered

1 lb fresh mushroom caps

1/2 c butter or margarine

2 lb venison loin; cut into 1 cubes

2 lg to 3 large tomatoessliced

2 md to 3 medium onionssliced

1 garlic salt to taste

1 pepper to taste

Saute green peppers and mushrooms in butter until crisp-tender; drain, reserving the butter.

Alternate meat and vegetables on skewers. Sprinkle with garlic salt and pepper. Grill kabobs about 6 inches over medium-hot coals 10 to 12 minutes or until done; basting with the reserved butter.

Yield: 6 to 8 servings.

Venison Kabobs 2

Yield: 8 servings

2 lb boneless venison sirloin;cut into 1-1/2 cubes

3 c vegetable oil

1/4 c dry burgundy

2 tb cider vinegar

1 1/2 tb liquid smoke

2 ts salt

1 ts white pepper

1 ts garlic powder

1 ts onion juice

16 ea cherry tomatoes

24 sm mushrooms

8 sm onions

2 lg green peppers; cut into

24-one-inch piec

1 hot cooked wild rice

Place meat in a shallow glass containerset aside.

Combine oil and next 7 ingredients; pour over meat. Cover and refrigerate 48 hours, stirring occasionally. Remove meat from marinade, reserving marinade.

Alternate meat and vegetables on skewers; brush with marinade. Grill kabobs over medium-hot coals 15 minutes, turning and basting frequently with marinade. Serve with wild rice.

Yield: 8 servings.

Venison Soup

Yield: 4 quarts

1 lb venison; cut into bite-sized- piece

1 ea 46-ounce can vegetable-cocktail juice (v-8)

1 ea 28-ounce can whole tomatoes; undrained and chopped

2 md red onions; chopped

1 tb worcestershire sauce

1/8 ts hot sauce

4 lg potatoes; peeled and cubed

3 md carrots sliced

4 sm yellow squash sliced

3 ea to 4 stalks celery; thinly-sliced

2 md green peppers; cut into 1 inch pieces

Combine first 6 ingredients in an 8-quart Dutch oven; bring to a boil. Reduce to medium heat; cover and cook 30 minutes, stirring occasionally. Stir in potatoes and carrots; cover and cook for 20 minutes.

Add remaining vegetables to soup; cook, uncovered, 10 additional minutes or until vegetables are crisp-tender.

Yield: 4 quarts.

Venison Tenderloin Appetizers

Categories: appetizers, game, southern

Yield: 15 appetizers

1 ea 1-1/2 to 2 pound venison-tenderloin

1/2 c red wine

2 tb olive oil

1 1/2 tb worcestershire sauce

1 ts dried whole thyme

3/4 ts onion powder

1/2 ts cumin seeds

1/4 ts pepper

1/8 ts ground cloves

1/8 ts garlic powder

Remove any white membrane surrounding tenderloin. Tie tenderloin with string, if necassary, to hold pieces of meat together. Place tenderloin in a shallow dish.

Combine wine, oil, and Worcestershire sauce; mix well. Add thyme and remaining ingredients, mixing well. Pour over tenderloin, and cover tightly. Refrigerate 8 hours, turning meat occasionally.

Remove tenderloin, reserving marinade. Place on a rack in a roasting pan; insert meat thermometer.

Bake at 425 degrees F for 30 minutes or until thermometer registers 160 degrees F (medium), basting occasionally with marinade. Allow meat to stand 10 minutes. Slice thinly with an electric knife. Serve with party rolls, mustard, and mayonnaise.

Yield: 15 appetizer servings.

Venison And Tomatoes

Yield: 4 servings

3 sl bacon; chopped

3/4 lb venison; ground

1/2 c onion; chopped

1 ts chili powder

3/4 ts salt

1/2 ts paprika

1/4 ts pepper

1 ea 14. 5 oz can stewed tomatoes

1 hot cooked rice

Fry bacon until crisp; add venison, onion, and seasonings. Cook over medium heat until meat is browned, stirring to crumble. Add tomatoes; cover, reduce heat, and simmer 40 minutes. Serve over rice.

Yield: 4 servings.

Country-Fried Venison

Yield: 6 servings

1 1/2 lb (3/4 thick) venison

1 c all-purpose flour

1 salt and pepper

1/4 ts seasoned salt

1/4 c bacon drippings

2 cl garlic; minced

4 c ; water

1/3 c all-purpose flour

1 1/2 ts bottled brown bouquet sauce

1 md onion; thinly sliced

1/2 lb fresh mushroomssliced

1 hot cooked rice

Prepare venison by trimming all fat and removing connective tissues. Cut meat into serving-size pieces, and pound each piece to 1/4-inch to 1/2-inch thickness. Combine 1 cup flour, 1/4 teaspoon salt, 1/8 teaspoon pepper, and seasoned salt; dredge the venison in flour mixture.

Heat 1 tablespoon bacon drippings in a large, heavy skillet; add garlic, and saute until golden. Remove garlic, and set aside. Add remaining bacon drippings to skillet; cook venison until it is lightly browned on both sides. Remove from skillet, and set aside.

Gradually stir about 1/2 cup water into 1/3 cup flour; mix until smooth, and add the remaining water. Stir flour mixture into pan drippings; cook over medium heat, stirring constantly, until thickened. Stir in bouquet sauce, 1/2 teaspoon salt, and 1/8 teaspoon pepper.

Return venison and garlic to skillet; reduce heat. Cover and simmer 30 minutes. Add onion; cover and simmer 15 minutes. Add mushrooms; cover and simmer 15 minutes. Serve over rice.

Yield: 6 servings.

Roast Haunch Of Venison

Categories: game, camping

Yield: 12 servings

1 no ingredients

1 six-pound haunch of Venison

1 Bottle claret or burgundy

1 large onion, sliced

1 bay leaf

1 crushed clove garlic

3 juniper berries

6 strips fat bacon - - - -

~ - ~ If the lower part of the leg is used, remove the shank bone from the venison. Place the meat in a large bowl, & marinate overnight in the wine with the Onion, Garlic, Bay Leaf & Juniper Berries.

Preheat oven to hot 450 degrees.

Remove the meat from the marinade & skewer & tie it into a compact shape. Strain and reservee the marinade. Insert a thermometer in the thickest portion of muscle & place the meat on a rack in an open roasting pan. Place the bacon strips on top of the meat.

Roas the meat twenty minutes. Reduce the oven temp. to moderate, 325 degrees & cook 15-18 min per pound to an internal temperature of 140 degrees for very rare; 150 degrees for medium-well done. While the meat is roasting, be sure to baste occasionally with the marinade. Serve with boiled potatoes, or as I use to, with boiled chestnuts.

Venison Steak St. Hubert

Categories: game, camping

Yield: 4 servings

1 no ingredients

4 Venison, round steaks - 8-9 oz. ea. , cut

1/2 - 3/4 " thick 2 shallots, chopped

2 carrots, sliced

2 onions, sliced

1 clove garlic, chopped

1/8 tsp. thyme

2 bay leaves

1/3 tsp freshly ground peper (I use mixture of white, black, red, green)

small pinch of ground cloves

2 cups dry, white wine

1 cup mild vinegar (3/4 C cider vinegar of 5% acidity, mixed with 1/4 C. water)

1/2 C. Olive Oil

Place the steaks in an enamel, glass or earthenwre bowl. Add the remaining ingredients, and allow to stand 24 hours in refrig. Turn the meat several times. Remove the steaks, and dry, reserving the marinade.

Saute the steaks in shallow, hot fat, until brown on both sides. The steaks should be rare. Serve on hot platter with sauce Poivrade (recipe to follow) SAUCE POIVRADE Yield approx 1. 5 C. 8 peppercorns, crushed 1/2 C. vinegar 2 tbsp red currant jelly 1 c. brown sauce, or leftover thickened gravy

Mix together peppercorns & vinegar, & simmer,

uncovered until reduced to 1/4 Cup.

Add brown sauce, and simmer 1/2 hour. Add Jelly. Strain, and serve over Venison Steaks

Venison Roast With Glaze

Yield: 4 servings

1 c orange juice

1 tb lemon juice

1 pn allspice

2 tb butter

2 tb orange juice

1/2 c crabapple or currant jelly

Smear roast with salt pork, season with salt and pepper and sear at 450 degrees for 15 minutes. Reduce oven to 325 degrees and cook, covered, for 12 minutes per pound, basting freq with a blend of oj, lemon juice and allspice. 20 minutes before roast is done, brush with glaze of 2 T oj, butter and jelly.

May be served with glazed orange and lemon slices, wild rice and mushrooms.

Venison Roast With Red Wine Gravy

Yield: 6 servings

3 lb to 5 lb venison roast

3 c red wine

2 lg onions; thinly sliced

12 ea black peppercorns

6 ea whole allspice

12 ea whole cloves

1 ea bay leaf

3 tb all purpose flour

1/4 c ; water

Remove any white membrane surrounding roast. Place roast in a shallow dish. Combine wine, onion, and seasonings. Pour over roast and cover. Marinate overnight in refrigerator, turning occasionally.

Remove roast from marinade, reserving marinade. Brown roast in a Dutch oven. Add marinade to roast, and bake, uncovered, at 350F for 1-1/2 hours or until meat thermometer registers 170F.

Remove bay leaf and discard. Remove roast, reserving marinade. Combine flour and water, stirring until smooth. Add flour mixture to marinade; cook over medium heat, stirring constantly, until thickened. Serve gravy with roast.

Yield: 6 to 8 servings.

Venison Roast

Yield: 8 servings

1 c ; water

1 c vinegar

2 ts salt

1/8 ts pepper

1 c dry red wine; divided

2 cl garlic

1 ea 3 to 5 pound venison roast

10 sl to 12 slices bacon

2 tb all purpose flour

2 c ; water

Combine 1 cup water, vinegar, salt, pepper, 3/4 cup wine, and garlic; pour over roast, and marinate overnight in refrigerator.

Drain roast, and place in a shallow roasting pan. Cover top of roast with bacon slices. Place aluminum foil over pan, and fold under to seal edges. Bake at 550 degrees F for 7 minutes. Reduce heat to 350 degrees F; bake for 1-1/2 hours, basting every 10 minutes with pan drippings.

Place flour in a skillet over medium heat; cook, stirring constantly, until lightly browned. Let cool. Combine 1/2 cup pan drippings, 2 cups water, and remaining 1/4 cup winestir well. Slowly add drippings mixture to flour; cook over medium heat, stirring constantly, until smooth. Serve gravy with roast.

Yield: 8 to 10 servings

Venison Chops Marchand De Muscadine

Yield: 4 servings

8 venison chops, 4 ounces each

1 1/4 ts tabasco pepper sauce

1 salt

1/4 lb butter or margarine, soften

1 tb vegetable oil

1/2 c sliced green onions

1 c dry white wine

1/2 c muscadine jelly

1/4 ts salt

1 chopped fresh parsley

Season the chops with 1 teaspoon of the Tabasco sauce and sprinkle them with salt. In a large skillet, melt 1 tablespoon of the butter and the oil over medium-high heat. In two batches, cook the chops for 5 minutes, turning once, and remove to a warm platter.

Melt 2 tablespoons of the butter in the same skillet. Add the green onions and cook, stirring frequently, for 3 minutes, or until tender. Stir in the wine. Bring to a boil and boil rapidly to reduce to 1/2 cup.

Stir in the jelly until it is melted. Add the remaining 1/4 teaspoon Tabasco sauce and salt to taste. Remove from the heat. Stir in the remaining 5 tablespoons butter, a tablespoon at a time, until the sauce is slightly thickened.

Serve over the chops. Sprinkle with parsley.

Venison Stew With Potato Dumplings

Yield: 8 servings

1/4 c shortening

1/4 c all-purpose flour

1 1/2 ts salt

10 1/2 oz can beef broth; undiluted

5 c ; water

2 tb lemon juice

1 md onionsliced

2 ea cloves

1 ea bay leaf

3 lb venison stew meat; cut into-1-1/2 pieces

1/2 c burgundy (optional)

2 lb potatoes; peeled

4 sl white bread

1 ts salt

1 tb onion; grated

1 ts parsley flakes

2 ea eggs; well beaten

1 all-purpose flour

Melt shortening in a large Dutch oven over low heat; add flour, stirring until roux is the color of caramel. Add 1-1/2 teaspoons salt and next 6 ingredients; boil 5 minutes. Add venison; cover, reduce heat, and simmer 2 hours. Add Burgundy, if desired.

Shred potatoes; drain well. Remove crust from bread,

and discard; tear bread into 1" pieces. Combine bread, potatoes, 1 teaspoon salt, 1 tablespoon onion, parsley, and eggs. Roll balls lightly in flour.

Drop dumplings into simmering stew. Cover, and cook over low heat 20 minutes or until dumplings are done. Remove bay leaf.

Yield: 8 servings.

Venison - Vegetable Bake

Yield: 8 servings

2 lb smoked venison sausage

1 sm onion; thinly sliced

14 1/2 oz can stewed tomatoes

1 ts dried whole oregano

1/4 ts pepper

4 md potatoes; thinly sliced

4 md carrots; thinly sliced

Remove casing from sausage, and discard. Brown meat in a large, lightly greased skillet over medium heat, stirring to crumble. Remove sausage, and drain well, reserving drippings in skillet. Saute onion in drippings; drain well, and discard drippings. Combine onion, tomatoes, oregano, and pepper in skillet. Simmer until thoroughly heated; remove from heat.

Arrange potatoes in a lightly greased 13" x 9" x 2" baking dish. Top with carrots. Sprinkle sausage over carrotsspoon tomato mixture over sausage.

Cover with aluminum foil. Bake at 350F for 45 minutes.

Yield: 8 servings.

Note: Thinly sliced Polish sausage may be substituted for venison sausage, if desired.

Sweet And Sour Sauce For Venison

Yield: 1 recipe

1 c catsup

1 c brown sugar

1/2 c vinegar

1/2 c water

2 or 3 bay leaves

1 dash of salt and pepper

1 sliced onion

2 to 4 lbs. of venison, chicken

1 or pork

Combine all ingredients and mix except onion. Pour over meat adding onion and cook covered at 350 degrees until meat is tender and sauce is thickened.

Venison Country Sausage

67 lb venison

33 lb pork

5 oz black pepper

30 oz salt

1 lb coriander

2 lg bulbs garlic, or to taste

Grind venison and pork after mixing with dry ingredients. Grend coarsely, not too fine. When ground, mix well, (fry a battie to taste). Stuff into casings (beef) and hang up to dry and smoke. Do not over smoke. Smoke slowly each day until desired smoke flavor is reached. If dry sausage is desired, allow to hang until thoroughly dry about 30 days or more. Place in freezing comppartment of freezer for another 30 days. Ready to eat as desired. If fresh sausage rather than smoked is desired, sausage mayy be kept frozen for a short pperiod of time and cooked as desired.

Brush Country Deer Loaf

Categories: game

Yield: 1 recipe

2 1/2 lb ground venison

1 md white onion

1 md bell pepper

2 eggs

1 c bread crumbs

1 cl garlic

3 tb chili powder

1 salt and pepper

1 10oz can tomato sauce

3 sl bacon

Mix first 8 ingredients--put in greased pyrex dish. Place bacon strips on topp of loaf. Pour tomato sauce over all. Bake in moderate oven 1 1/2 hours or until done.

Venison Sauce Piquante

Categories: game

Yield: 1 recipe

4 lb round of venison, cut in 1-2 cubes

8 md onions, chopped

2 bn chopped green onions

1 lg chopped bell pepper

1 c chopped celery

2 8 oz. cans tomato sauce and

1 paste

1 c olive oil

2 cl garlic, chopped

2 tb worcestershire sauce

1 juice of two lemons

3/4 c bacon drippings

1 c flour (for roux)

1 salt, black pepper and

1 red cayenne pepper

6 c water

Wash venison, season with salt and pepper, and fry in bacon drippings, until brown. Remove from fat and set aside. Using olive oil and flour, make a roux with tomato sauce and paste. To make a roux--Cover bottom of heavy pot with olive oil. After the olive oil is well heated over a slow fire, add the flour. Cook the flour very slowly, stirring almost constantly. The flour must be browned to a very dark brown, nearly black, but not actually burned. Add a small can of tomato paste, stirring this all the time until the roux has reached the color of the flour before the papste was added. Then add a small can of tomato sauce, stirring this into the mixture until it all turns dark brown again. Add all chopped seasoning, except garlic, cover and simmer on low heat for about 1 hour. Add venison to roux and chopped seasoning mixture. Simmer for 30 minutes covered. Add water and garlic, cover and let cook slowly for about 2 hours. Serve over rice or spaghetti.

Venison Marinade

Categories: game

Yield: 1 recipegs

1 salt

1 pepper, coarse ground

1 worchestershire sauce

2 tb lemon juice

1/2 c clear italian dressing

1 bay leaves

1 thin sliced onion

1 garlic, minced (optional)

Slice meat in 1/2" slices. Place in bowl, add 1 T. salt, enough water to cover, cover with lid and place in refrigerator. Next day, drain liquid, add salt again, water and soak. Repeat this pprocess for 3 to 5 days. On the 5th day, drain meat, rinse and dry with a paper towel. In a shallow pan, place meat, spprinkle with pepper (it has already been salted) and rub each with worchestershire sauce. Place meat in single layer in ppan and sprinkle over meat: lemon juice, italian dressing, garlic, onion, and bay leaves. Soak over-night, turning several times. To barbeque, baste with marinade. To pan fry, drain meat, blot with paper towels, then beat in flour and fry.

Venison With Forest Berry Relish

Categories: game

Yield: 4 servings

1 no ingredients

Lard a 1. 5 kg saddle of venison generously with 200 g smoked bacon cut into thin strips. Mix a few crushed black peppers, juniper berries and coriander seed with 5 cl oil, 2 tablespoons od mustard and salt and spread on meat.

Slice 2 onions and heap on the meat, wrap in foil and leave to stand for 2 days. Before cooking, wipe the spices off the meat, brush lightly with oil, roast for 25-30 minutes in a hot oven until medium done, slice and rearrange the meat on the bone to serve. Accompany with stewed onf preserved fruit.

Venison Scallopini

Categories: game

Yield: 4 servings

1 lb venison, cut into cubes

1/8 ts freshly ground black pepper

1/4 cup vegetable oil

1/2 ts garlic, minced

3 oz can sliced mushrooms

1/4 ts oregano

1/2 ts salt

1 tb flour

1 medium onion, thinly sliced 3 cans tomato sauce (8 oz cans) 1 tb parsley, finely chopped hot noodles

Heat oil in medium sized skillet. Sprinkle venison with flour, salt & pepper. Add venison to hot oil and brown slowly. Remove venison from skillet. Add garlic and onion to skillet, cooking until tender. Add venison and all remaining ingredients except noodles. Cover and simmer 25 minutes. Serve over hot noodles.

Venison Civet

Yield: 6 servings

1 1/2 kg venisonstewing

--FOR MARINADE--

200 g onionsliced

1 shallot sliced

100 g carrot sliced

2 garlic cloves

1 parsley stalks

1 herbes de provence or thyme

1 salt

1 peppercorns; lightly crushed

30 ml cognac or good armagnac

1 l red wine; good - or to cove 50 ml oil, just to cover

1 juniper berries

----TO COOK

200 g pork back fat

100 g cooking fat/oil

200 g onion

50 g flour

500 ml red wine; good

1 salt

1 pepper

----OPTIONAL----

1 garlic clove; crushed

10 ml vinegar

100 ml blood, to thicken

Compose marinade. Slice onions, carrots, shallots & garlic, add herbs and spices and cognac or armagnac. Add meat cut into largeish pieces, now pour over enough wine to cover meat, Marinade meat 2 days, stirring morning & night.

The day before serving, Take out and put into sieve, rejecting the vegetables. cut back fat into dice and fry in cooking fat. Add onion, (optional, when cooked take it out, liquidise and return) Fry meat in this fat until it becomes grey - it won't brown because it was marinaded.

Sprinkle over the flour and stir till it disappears. Heat cooking wine (corbi*res) pour delicately over meat, stirring to incorporate flour. Add enough to cover the meat. Simmer until meat is very nearly tender. Allow to cool.

On the day of the meal, remove excess fat, reheat and simmer until meat is falling off bones. Strain sauce and reduce if needed. Add marinade - stirring. Correct seasoning. Add optional garlic, and a dash of vinegar if needed, reheat to simmering point. If using blood, add it to simmering sauce off the heat, stirring the while. Pour back over the meat and serve without re-heating.

Old Man Kelsey's Deer Jerky

Categories: game, preserves, dehydrator

Yield: 1 servings

1 1/2 to 2 lbs lean boneless deer-meat, partially frozen

1/4 c soy sauce

1 tb worcestershire sauce

1/4 ts ground pepper

1/4 ts garlic powder

1/4 ts onion powder

1/4 ts hickory smoked salt

1/4 c firmly packed brown sugar

1 sm bottle liquid smoke

Trim all fat from the meat. Slice the meat as thinly as possible. In a bowl combine the remaining ingredients. Stir until dissolved. Add the meat and mix well. Cover and refrigerate overnight. Shake the excess liquid from the meat and arrange in a shallow pan or cookie sheet. Dry the meat in a 150F or 200F oven until dry and brown, a minimum of 8 hours. Cool, remove from the pan, and store in a glass jar.

NOTE If spicy hot jerky is desired, you may sprinkle coarsely ground black pepper over the meat just before placing it in the oven.

Spiced Venison Roast

Yield: 1 recipe

Rub salt and peper into roast. Place in self basting pot and lay slices of onion over entire topp. Cover onions with strips of bacon; top bacon with chopped celery including some tops. Hold in place with toothpicks. Pour a Coca-cola over the roast; cover and roast at

350 degrees until tender.

Roast Rack Of Venison With Wild Mushrooms

2 tb olive oil

1 2 3/4-lb rack of venison, trimmed, ; boned, bones rese

1 sm onion, chopped

1 sm leek, chopped

1 carrot, chopped

4 c water

1 1/2 c dry red wine

1 c canned low salt chicken broth

1 c canned beef broth

2 bay leaves

1 sprig fresh thyme

1 garlic clove, chopped

6 juniper berries

6 whole black peppercorns

8 tb (1 stick) chilled butter

1 lb fresh wild mushrooms, stemmed, capssliced

Heat oil in heavy large Dutch oven over medium heat. Add bonessaute until beginning to brown, about 10 minutes. Add onion, leek and carrotsaute until golden, about 15 minutes. Add 4 C water, wine, both broths, bay leaves, thyme, garlic, juniper berries and peppercorns. Bring to boil, scraping up any browned bits. Reduce heat to medium lowsimmer 1 1/2 hours, skimming occasionally. Strain into heavy medium saucepan. Boil until reduced to 3/4 C, about 25 minutes. Season with salt and pepper.

Preheat oven to 425'F. Melt 2 T butter in heavy large

ovenproof skillet over medium-high heat. Season venison with salt and pepper. Add to skillet; brown on all sides, about 8 minutes. Transfer swiet to oven; roast venison until thermometer inserted into thickest part registers 130'F for medium rare, about 15 minutes. Transfer to platter; tent with foil.

Melt 2 T butter in same skillet over medium-high heat. Add mushroomssaute until tender about 5 minutes. Season with salt and pepper.

Bring sauce to simmer. Remove from heat. Add remaining 4 T butter, 1 T at a time, whisking just until melted. Serve venison with mushrooms and sauce.

Gene Blystone's Venison Mincemeat

Yield: 1 servings

4 lb venison

2 lb beef suet tart apples

3 lb brown sugar

2 c maple syrup or 2 c dark molasses

2 qt cider

3 lb currants

4 lb seeded raisins

1/2 lb citron, cut fine

1 qt brandy or 1 qt wine

1 tb cinnamon

1 tb ground clove

1 ts allspice

1 ts mace

1 ts nutmeg salt to taste apple-jack or

Cover and cook the venison and suet with boiling water until tender; let it cool in the liquid. When it is cold and the fat has solidified, remove meat and chop the cake fat (suet). Reboil the liquid until it has been reduced to 1 1/2 cups. Chop the venison and add it to twice as much peeled, cored and finely chopped apple. Add the sugar and maple syrup or molasses. Add the dried fruit, suet, cider and the reduced boiling liquid. Boil slowly for 2 hours, stirring to prevent burning. Add the apple jack or brandy or wine and the spices. Mix thoroughly and store in crocks or jars. May also be frozen, but does't freeze hard.

Yield: 15 pies, recipe can be cut in half.

Note: It is by no means necessary to use exactly the ingredients given. You may want to add orange or lemon peel, chopped figs or may prefer a different proportion of spices. You may also use wine or sherry in place of the cider.

Loin Of Venison With Cherry Chile Salsa

Yield: 4 servings

1 venison loin (or 2 lb 1 backstrap)

1/2 c apple cider

2 c dried cherries

1 pear, finely chopped 1 (unpeeled)

1/2 c peeled, diced jicama

1 c-cleaned, ; roasted green

1 chiles

Oven Temp: 400oF 1. Preheat oven to 400F. Rinse and dry the venison. Tie with a string so that it is of uniform thickness. Lightly season with salt and pepper. Heat a saute pan with a thin coating of olive oil.

2. When the oil is hot, brown the venison on all sides, then place the venison in the oven for 15 to 20 minutes, until medium rare. Allow the venison to sit at room temperature for at least 20 minutes before slicing thinly to serve.

3. Place apple cider in a small saucepan over moderate heat. Add dried cherries and remove from heat when liquid is hot, not boiling. Cover pan with lid and set aside, off heat, until cherries are plumped and soft, about 20 minutes.

4. Add chopped pear, jicama and chilies to cherries. There should be little or no liquid left in pan; drain if necessary.

Deer Pemican (Ogalala Sioux)

Put clean dried meat in bread pan and roast; when ready, sprinkle some water on the roasted meat, cool, wrapp meat in a clean white cloth and pound until meat is real tender and flaky; add tallow grease, and sugar and raisins to taste.

Delaware Indian Deer Liver With Onions

Yield: 1 recipe

1 venison liver, sliced

3 c water

4 tb flour

1/2 ts salt

1/2 c dry red wine

1/4 ts pepper

4 tb bacon fat

2 c wild onions, sliced

1 can mushroom soup

1 can water

Trim and wash the liver and slice into 1/4" slices. Pour half of the boiling water over the slices, drain and pat dry. Reepat. On a platter, mix the flour, salt and peppper. Dredge the liver in the flour mixture. Over high heat, heat the bacon fat until blue smoke appears.

Add the liver and saute on both sides until lightly browned. Remove the liver with a slotted spoon and set aside.

Add the thinly sliced onions and cook until golden brown. Be careful not to burn the onions. Lower the heat, add the mushroom soup, one can of warm water and the liver. Cover and cook for 1 1/2 hours, making sure that the pan does not cook dry. Add 1/2 c. wine just before the liver is ready. Served with mashed potatoes and melted bacon grease as gravy.

Kiowa Venison Roast

1 slab of venison, about 2, 1 thick

4 ts bacon fat

1/4 ts pepper

1 tb celery, chopped

1/2 c flour

1/2 ts salt

1 tb onion, chopped

2 c water, boiling

Lay venison on board and pound flour into it. Melt fat in a large frying pan, and brown roast in it. Add all the seasoning and 1/2 of the water. Cover and let simmer for 55 minutes. Pour in rest of water and simmer until done.

Bill's Venison Roast

Soak roast overnight in saltwater. Rinse and dry off. Cut slits in top side of roast about 2-3 inches apart, depending on how spicy you want it. Alternate 1/2 clove of garlic and slices of green serano or jalapeno peppers. Turn the roast over, repeat. Do not add spices or salt.

Cover roast HEAVILY all over with cheap prepared mustard. Put in dry pan.

Cover heavily with yellow onion sliced in rings. Cover. Put in preheated 300 degree oven. Roast til it's really tender, slice across grain, serve with brown or wild rice and greens.

Venison Etouffee

5 lb venison, cut

1/2 inch cubes

1 onion (equal meat in volume)

1 c fine chopped bell pepper

1/2 ea lemon, chopped fine

2 ts garlic, chopped fine

1 louisiana hot sauce to taste

1 salt to taste

2 tb worcestershire sauce

1 c chopped fresh parsley

1 olive oil

Salt and pepper meat and brown in olive oil. Put in heavy pot with all other ingredients. Cook on low heat from 6 to 8 hours until venison is tender. Serve over rice. Do not add any other liquids, but stir occasionally. For measuring the onions, by volume, we mean if you have a cup of meat, then you need a cup of onions.